OLD TESTAMENT MESSAGE

A Biblical-Theological Commentary

Carroll Stuhlmueller, C.P. and Martin McNamara, M.S.C.
EDITORS

Old Testament Message, Volume 17

PROVERBS

with an
Introduction to Sapiential Books

Dermot Cox, O.F.M.

Michael Glazier, Inc.
Wilmington, Delaware

First published in 1982 by: MICHAEL GLAZIER, INC., 1723 Delaware Avenue, Wilmington, Delaware 19806
Distributed outside U.S., Canada & Philippines by: GILL & MACMILLAN, LTD., Goldenbridge, Inchicore, Dublin 8 Ireland

Library of Congress Catalog Card Number: 81-85271
International Standard Book Number
Old Testament Message series: 0-89453-235-9
PROVERBS
0-89453-251-0 (Michael Glazier, Inc.)
7171-1181-4 (Gill & MacMillan, Ltd.)

Cover design by Lillian Brulc

Printed in the United States of America

Contents

The Book of Proverbs

Book I
The Proverbs of Solomon
Son of David
1:1—9:18

Book III
The Words of the Wise
22:17—24:22

Book IV
The Collection of Proverbs Made For Hezekiah
25:1—29:27

Book V
Four Appendices
30:1—31:31

Editors' Preface

Old Testament Message brings into our life and religion today the ancient word of God to Israel. This word, according to the book of the prophet Isaiah, had soaked the earth like "rain and snow coming gently down from heaven" and had returned to God fruitfully in all forms of human life (Isa 55:10). The authors of this series remain true to this ancient Israelite heritage and draw us into the home, the temple and the marketplace of God's chosen people. Although they rely upon the tools of modern scholarship to uncover the distant places and culture of the biblical world, yet they also refocus these insights in a language clear and understandable for any interested reader today. They enable us, even if this be our first acquaintance with the Old Testament, to become sister and brother, or at least good neighbor, to our religious ancestors. In this way we begin to hear God's word ever more forcefully in our own times and across our world, within our prayer and worship, in our secular needs and perplexing problems.

Because life is complex and our world includes, at times in a single large city, vastly different styles of living, we have much to learn from the Israelite Scriptures. The Old Testament spans forty-six biblical books and almost nineteen hundred years of life. It extends through desert, agricultural and urban ways of human existence. The literary style embraces a world of literature and human emotions. Its history began with Moses and the birth-pangs of a new people, it came of age politically and economically under David and Solomon, it reeled under the fiery threats of prophets like Amos and Jeremiah. The people despaired and yet were re-created with new hope during the Babylonian exile. Later reconstruction in the homeland and then the trauma of apocalyptic movements prepared for the revelation of "the mystery hidden for ages in God who created all things" (Eph 3:9).

While the Old Testament telescopes twelve to nineteen hundred years of human existence within the small country of Israel, any single moment of time today witnesses to the reenactment of this entire history across the wide expanse of planet earth. Each verse of the Old Testament is being relived somewhere in our world todav. We need, therefore, the *entire* Old Testament and all twenty-three volumes of this new set, in order to be totally a "Bible person" within today's widely diverse society.

The subtitle of this series—"A Biblical-Theological Commentary"—clarifies what these twenty-three volumes intend to do.

Their *purpose* is theological: to feel the pulse of God's word for its *religious* impact and direction.

Their *method* is biblical: to establish the scriptural word firmly within the life and culture of ancient Israel.

Their *style* is commentary: not to explain verse by verse but to follow a presentation of the message that is easily understandable to any serious reader, even if this person is untrained in ancient history and biblical languages.

Old Testament Message—like its predecessor, *New Testament Message*—is aimed at the entire English-speaking world and so is a collaborative effort of an international team. The twenty-one contributors are women and men drawn from North America, Ireland, Britain and Australia. They are scholars who have published in scientific journals, but they have been chosen equally as well for their proven ability to communicate on a popular level. This twenty-three book set comes from Roman Catholic writers, yet, like the Bible itself, it reaches beyond interpretations restricted to an individual church and so enables men and women rooted in biblical faith to unite and so to appreciate their own traditions more fully and more adequately.

Most of all, through the word of God, we seek the blessedness and joy of those

who walk in the law of the Lord!...
who seek God with their whole heart (Ps. 119:1-2).

Carroll Stuhlmueller, C.P. *Martin McNamara, M.S.C.*

INTRODUCTION TO SAPIENTIAL LITERATURE

CHAPTER 1.
THE NATURE OF WISDOM.

An innate desire to know and to dominate the environment is a basic characteristic of humankind, and to this the sapiential literature responds. It inculcates "wisdom", and wisdom is the ability to achieve mastery of life, to establish values, to acquire skills.

At different times in mankind's history this process may have been determined by particular needs—survival, administration, social life, religious commitment—but essentially the goal remained the same; the sage was, above all else, a believer in human dignity and a proponent of human values: one who sought to acquire and communicate "wisdom".

Indeed wisdom, as it is seen in the Bible, is a quality of mind and spirit that directs all human activity towards its proper end. One possessed *hokmâ,* wisdom, when one's way of life was lived in accordance with mature standards, which were in turn derived from experience and intelligence, secular and religious. The Law and the Prophets inculcate a way of life, it is true, but in fact one lives for the most part an everyday existence in the world, and there are many aspects of daily life that evade the broader categories of revealed religion. So the key to success and virtue, the stepping-stone to "goodness", is wisdom, which enables one to dominate the ordinary environment of life. This is the goal of all human knowledge and skill, and it determines the sapiential literature of Israel.

The Wisdom Literature of Israel

Even within the context of the Old Testament it is not always easy to define the term "Wisdom literature." Too often it is an indeterminate classification, sometimes identified by its similarity to extra-biblical literature, sometimes by reference to its obvious international character, or even its typical lack of interest in such otherwise central themes as covenant and salvation-history.

In fact, under the rather ill-fitting label "wisdom" come many kinds of writings: artistic, didactic, meditative. One meets people who teach, pray, or find both pleasure and amusement in literary creation. This naturally results in a more broad-minded and artistic approach to life, even religious life—a blend of humanism and faith. What distinguishes it from the rest of the Old Testament tradition is its didactic nature, and its emphasis on the human and secular side of life. It believes that mankind and the world are capable of improvement, and are improvable by purely human effort. Mankind can affect its environment, and by faith even transcend it.

> yes, if you cry out for insight
> and raise your voice for understanding,
> if you seek it like silver
> and search for it as for hidden treasures;
> then you will understand the fear of the Lord
> and find the knowledge of God.
>
> (Prov 2:3–5)

Proverbs understands this insight (see below, p. 109). It is this human dimension that makes the sapiential literature part of the world of international scholarship.

This may explain the attribution of much of the wisdom literature (Proverbs, Qoheleth, Canticle and Wisdom of Solomon) to Solomon. In the tradition he is regarded as the "founder" of wisdom, though most of the material can safely be dated later than the tenth century B.C. when he ruled. Undoubtedly, he had an interest in wisdom, and this may well have stemmed from the international flavour of his policy (see 1 Kgs 4:29; 5:1–18; 10:1–22; 11:1–8 for example). The sapiential tradition was strong in Canaan before Israel settled in the land, and it is possible that Solomon adopted it along with his government structures. It was an age noticeably concerned with secular relations and with the international scene.

Only three Old Testament books are universally accepted as wisdom in character: Proverbs, Qoheleth and Job. However, it is more generally accepted that the Canticle of Canticles, Sirach and Wisdom also form part of the sapiential tradition. To this we may add several psalms or parts of psalms—1; 32(31); 34(33); 37(36); 49(48); 73(72); 112(111); 128(127); and some fragments of texts, such as Bar 3:9—4:14 and isolated sections of Tobit. The traditional classification according to the Hebrew canon—called *ketubîm* or "Writings"—is shorter, but more clearly established, and consists of Job, Psalms (or "praises"), Proverbs, Qoheleth and Canticle of Canticles.

Israel's Wisdom literature is distinguished from the rest of the biblical tradition in that it prescinds from the purely religious tradition of "People of God" and concerns itself with the individual—and individual needs and aims. Most of the Old Testament literature is concerned with salvation history and the unique status of a covenant people. There are, indeed, different ways of viewing this, but the essential "salvation-orientation" remains. In Wisdom much of the distinctive "Israelite" concern is lacking, or at least underplayed. (Sirach however has a special interest in both Wisdom and *Tôrah*.) Election, covenant, law and cult are scarcely mentioned. Qoheleth affords an example, with his rather offhand reference to established religion:

> Guard your steps when you go near the house of God;
> to draw near to listen is better than to offer the sacrifice
> of fools; for they do not know that they are doing evil.
> Be not rash with your mouth, nor let your heart be hasty

> to utter a word before God, for God is in heaven, and you upon earth.
>
> (Qoh 5:1–2).

This is a far cry from the religious exhortation of covenant religion, as is Qoh 7:16:

> Be not righteous overmuch, and do not make yourself overwise; why should you destroy yourself?

Even the name of God is the general term for the *deity,* rather than the personal name of Yahweh, except in some few texts in Proverbs and the last part of Job (and even in these cases the context is seldom if ever that of the covenant relationship between Yahweh and his people). This is not to say that the wisdom writers were not concerned with religious matters, but that they had wider interests, and this fact is reflected in a type of literature that is more self-consciously secular and intellectual than religious. There was good reason for this preoccupation. As Israel evolved from desert to urban establishment, to exile and back, life became more complex and situations arose that were not adequately served by the more overtly theological literature. So the sage was forced more and more to fall back on experience and intelligence. Since this process is shared by all literate peoples, Wisdom takes on a wider perspective than either Law or Prophets, bringing to the Old Testament tradition a richness found nowhere else in the Bible.

Given this variety and scope in the sapiential tradition it may be best to proceed from the nature of the wisdom project to define the literature. The sage is primarily interested in the human person as such, and with the moral order, rather than with historical events. So the most important question that Wisdom asks is—how, practically, can one achieve human fulfillment, that is, both worldly and moral success? This is more or less the same sort of question asked by people in all human circumstances and in all ages, and the answer is found in a knowledge of human nature and the nature of the world.

> What is man, and of what use is he?
> What is his good, and what is his evil?

This basic question, asked here by Sir 18,8, is found also in Job 7:17, and runs like a refrain through Qoheleth, where the human world comes under a sceptical gaze:

> I have seen the business that God has given to the sons of men to be busy with. He has made everything beautiful in its time; also he has put eternity into man's mind, yet so that he cannot find out what God has done from the beginning to the end.
>
> (Qoh 3:10–11).

See also Qoh 1:3–11; 2:1–23. From such knowledge, if once one reaches it, one can evolve rules of comportment to enable man to live in the world. Since this world of the Old Testament was a world of believers, one further question had to be put—and answered: the nature of God's relationship with the human ambient.

In a word, the sapiential literature is interested in getting the individual to think about existence and to achieve something humanly valuable. The stages of its development can, to some extent at least, be traced in the pages of the Old Testament. From the very beginning we find practical, concrete wisdom, interested in man and his world—how to watch the seasons, how and when to plant and reap; how to observe the changing political scene and be a competent administrator. Much of the material in the earlier strata of Proverbs (10:1—22:16 and 25:1—29:27 for example) is of this kind. The process of observation and thought became more organized in books such as Wisdom and Sirach, as a "science of humanity", in which one finds more thoughtful orientations for life, a life that can truly be called human. Wis 8:17–21 describes the ideal:

> When I considered these things inwardly,
> and thought upon them in my mind,
> that in kinship with wisdom there is immortality,
> and in friendship with her, pure delight,
> and in the labours of her hands, unfailing wealth,
> and in the experience of her company, understanding,
> and renown in sharing her words,
> I went about seeking how to get her for myself.
> (vv. 17–18)

Concomitant with this is a more sophisticated interest in the manner in which theology impinges upon the human environment—for God, too, is a phenomenon of experience (Job and Qoheleth).

Thus, possibly the better definition of sapiential literature, if one is needed, is "civilized" literature, the writings of cultured and civilized people, regarding their society, their world and their view of human life in general—in other words, it is a literature whose primary concern is human life and nature, and the individual's evaluation of them based on experience and reason.

Indeed, a very good rule is not to try to define it too strictly—a wisdom style crops up in the most unexpected places: among the Midrash (Tobit), the Apocrypha (Baruch) and in poetry (Psalms). If it is possible to find a common denominator it is its didactic, international and empiric nature. "Where is the place of understanding?", Job rightly asks (28:12), and is very careful not to answer too strictly. Indeed, it is not too easily determined either by time or place. Clearly, the question of "what *is* wisdom?" is much more open in the Old Testament than later ages admit, as the scope of wisdom was broader than any one discipline now allows. This is borne out by the "curriculum" of the learned that we find in Sirach and Daniel (see below, p. 33). It was concerned with human life, with understanding this, and enabling one to live successfully and well on the terrestrial plane. It sets out to inculcate practical worldly wisdom, savoir-faire, and where relevant the religious virtues; a concern for human values—freedom, justice, reward and punishment, suffering—and an awareness of the mystery that lies at the root of things.

The Poetic Expression of Wisdom.

Wisdom adopts different modes of expression for different peoples: to the Greeks, the tragic expression of myth—stories that symbolize mankind's mysterious involvement with the universe; to Egyptians and Babylonians, instruction and dialogue that enabled man to harmonize existence with an often arbitrary cosmic order; to the Israelite the mode was instruction, proverb, dialogue and myth, an adapted form of which can be found for instance in the *Book of Job.* In each case, the medium is symbolic language, the use of imagery.

This has one important result that must be borne in mind: Wisdom in Israel is for the most part written in poetry, so poetic hermeneutics, or interpretative art, determine the meaning. The type of poetry found in the books of wisdom, and in the Old Testament, is different from what we know as poetry, having neither the metric structure nor the rhyme that dominates our western tradition. Instead, it is based on a system of accents and beats, and on parallelism. In fact, since the Hebrew text as it stands is relatively recent, it is not always possible to be sure of the accent, so it is often better to rely on the general "feel" of the rhythm, which can be *binary, ternary* or *quaternary* (having two, three or four beats). The line of poetry is the basic unit, and is known as the stich, and this can be divided into two sub-units (a distich) or three sub-units (a tristich). Thus one can come across a proverb or a "verse" of poetry composed of two or three parts.

The most important aspect of the poetry one finds in the Old Testament is what has traditionally been called "parallelism". This is a balance of rhythm and ideas. There are three basic kinds: *synonymous parallelism* is found where two lines share the same thought, the second repeating the first, as in Ps 49:1:

> Hear this, all peoples!
> Give ear, all inhabitants of the world;

antithetic parallelism holds up a contrast of opposite, or antithetic ideas, such as is found in Prov 10:1:

> A wise son makes a glad father,
> but a foolish son is a sorrow to his mother;

synthetic parallelism is a rather general label that is used to cover types of parallelism that do not readily fit into either of the other categories, the second stich normally supplementing the first in some way or another as in a progression of ideas such as one finds in Ps 1:1:

> Blessed is the man
> who walks not in the counsel of the wicked,
> nor stands in the way of sinners,
> nor sits in the seat of scoffers.

Other poetic forms frequently found are *acrostic* poems, in which verses begin with successive letters of the alphabet, an example of which is Prov 31:10–31.

The predominant use of poetry in the sapiential literature means one thing in particular—it is frequently existential in its impact on the listener or reader, due to the subjective element one finds in poetry. Prov 25:2 affords a good example. In itself it has a particular meaning, but as a statement it is open enough to mean different things to different readers, as a comparison of Tob 12:7 and the interpretation found below, p. 210f, bears out. Wisdom thus becomes the expression of encounter with truth, an encounter with life and with experience. The mode that the sapiential literature adopts is, as it were, existentialism become abstract. Job's experience of the absurdity of life, for example, begins as a very personal perception of a very individual person, but is transmuted by dramatic poetry into a general appreciation of the absurdity of all human life. In its primary perception, therefore, Wisdom is experiential and individual; in communication it is highly stylized. It must be approached as one approaches poetry.

In practical terms, the sages reflected on human experience, and transmitted their appreciation of it with a view of making liveable both social life and individual life. In this way the sages arrived at a concept of "wisdom dialectic", a confrontation between experience and tradition that often leads the thinker beyond the original bounds of experience, and enables him to transcend the limits of the known. What distinguishes their work is the desire for rational clarification, and the ordering of the world of their experience.

> Three things are too wonderful for me;
> four I do not understand:
> the way of an eagle in the sky,
> the way of a serpent on a rock,
> the way of a ship on the high seas,
> and the way of a man with a maiden.
>
> (Prov 30:18–19)

This is a fine example of the dialectic at work. The mystery of human sexuality is indeed imposing (v. 19). By comparing experiences of the mysterious in other fields and leaving the comparison open-ended, the author stimulates the reader or listener to draw, in turn, his own comparisons and subsequent conclusions. This is in fact the task of the sage—to pin down the order and function of the perceptible in natural phenomena and in human life, so as to evolve a ruling principle. For the reader, the essential discipline is to take the author's perception *as a starting point* for one's own excogitation. A wisdom statement is seldom an object fully specified in itself. The maxim, and indeed the more evolved dialogue mode, only functions in controlling a given experience according to the intellectual preconceptions (literary and cognitive) of the user. This is why *parallelism* is so frequently used in poetry. The writer can give expression to the subject matter from two points of view, in two verse lines, so as to provoke thought rather than supply answers:

> A false balance is an abomination to the Lord,
> but a just weight is his delight.
> When pride comes, then comes disgrace;
> but with the humble is wisdom.
> The integrity of the upright guides them,
> but the crookedness of the treacherous destroys them.
> Riches do not profit on the day of wrath,
> but righteousness delivers from death.
>
> (Prov 11:1–4)

So in fact what wisdom poetry sets out to do is not so much to communicate a precise concept or judgement, prepackaged as it were, but to reproduce the value of an experience. The knowledge spoken of by the Wisdom literature is not a simple approach to objects that accords the reader a passive role as recipient. It compels a positive attitude and so determines the level at which life is to be lived. This extends to human relationships, which are also a sapiential preoccupation. Here again is found an underlying acceptance of the fact that this is to some extent one's own affair—how one chooses to go about it must be determined by one's own judgement of the circumstances. The reader's autonomy in this matter is paramount to the proverbial literature. Here we find seemingly contradictory maxims side by side, and it is clearly up to the reader to decide what his or her own reaction should be.

> The poor is disliked even by his neighbour,
> but the rich has many friends.
> He who despises his neighbour is a sinner,
> but happy is he who is kind to the poor.

This example comes from Prov 14:20–21, but even Qoh 5:7–12 retains the faint resonance of this principle of autonomous judgement.

To the wise, teaching is never indoctrination; the pupil may not just passively *receive* a doctrine from the teacher—his own intellect must be actively involved. The pupil must personally determine the relative importance, in his circumstances, of each point being taught—and decide on its validity. The ideal pupil-teacher attitude could be described as "balanced contestation", based on the disparity of experience.

Wisdom's Theological Standpoint.

The authority of the sage, like that of the prophet and priest, derived ultimately from God (cf. Jer 8:8–9; Ezek 7:26), and even the prophet has been known to give "counsel" (as in Isa 6), which is often taken to be the sage's prerogative. Both prophecy and wisdom are divine gifts, but the concerns of wisdom differ from those of prophecy, as did the way they went to work.

The sages began with the belief that the world was essentially ordered and good, and that inherent to the nature of things was a divine order that could be comprehended by human effort. Thus the bedrock of the sapiential tradition is simply a belief that mankind has been so created and commissioned by God that the right use of human faculties can enable one to achieve "life". Man need not, therefore, continually refer beyond himself and his world for answers. Qoheleth's point of departure is usually "what he has seen" and experienced—Qoh 1:12–14, 17; 2:1–3; 3:16; 4:1–4; 5:13 etc., and even the wisdom psalms proceed from the same argument—Ps 73(72); 49(48) for example. Armed with wisdom, the human being can assume responsibility for, and attain mastery over, creation. Indeed, from the Old Testament point of view, wisdom is in a sense a theology of creation, the affinity between the Wisdom tradition and the priestly tradition of Gen 1 is remarkable. In the first chapter of Genesis the human person is created "in the image of God", and the emphasis is laid in a noticeable way on the fact that this divine likeness resides in mankind's dominion over the created world (an insight lacking in the parallel Yahwist tradition of Gen 2, see below, p. 35). It is essentially a human phenomenon—at its most fundamental it represents the human creature assessing his own situation, and articulating that assessment in a more or less consciously artistic manner.

While it is tied to, and for the most part remains loyal to, the biblical faith, Wisdom literature emphasises one particular aspect—mankind in its secular, terrestrial existence, as the human person confronts the material world, human history and existence, and wrests meaning and value from them at the everyday level. While this secular aspect is dominant, especially in older wisdom (such as Proverbs), the god-experience naturally exerts its own pressure, for ultimately God is controller of creation.

Consequently, Old Testament Wisdom has a special way of looking at the individual. He is not so much a recipient of divine intervention or revelation as an active, quasi-autonomous collaborator in what is happening on the earthly scene. This is his special role in the eyes of the sages:

> The Lord created man out of earth,
> and turned him back to it again.
> He gave to men few days, a limited time,
> but granted them authority over the things upon
> the earth.
> He endowed them with strength like his own,
> and made them in his own image.
> He placed the fear of them in all living beings,
> and granted them dominion over beasts and birds.

This text from Sir 17:1–4 is echoed in Wis 10:2, and especially Wis 9:2:

and by thy wisdom hast formed man,
to have dominion over the creatures thou hast made
and rule the world in holiness and righteousness.

The echo of Gen 1 resounds in these texts. By understanding his place in the world, by realizing his role as master of creation, the individual controls the material universe, and by control creates it. Thus to a marked degree Wisdom offers a theology of the human person, quite often secular in its interests. Whatever interest it shows in ethics is in worldly, or at least human, ethics—the natural law (see below, p. 71). This is a result of the fact that Wisdom is essentially empirical, emphasizing what can be deduced from natural phenomena, and to the fact that it is bounded by life on earth. Death is seen as the ultimate end of all living creatures (cf. Qoh 2:15; Sir 44:9; Wis 2:2–4). Except for the Book of Wisdom, last on the scene in the first century B.C., there is no belief in an afterlife, so everything had to be worked out within the limits of this world.

This results in a special way of approaching the practicalities of life—statecraft, professional activity, the business of running one's daily life. Sapiential texts show a real interest in affairs—human, political, commercial. Neither revelation nor covenant is seen as a source of motivation or guidance, except peripherally. Rather is emphasis laid on the human ability to think things through and impose rational order on life. Indeed, one central intuition that we find in sapiential literature is its belief in, and emphasis on, common humanity. The enrichment of the human person in its totality remains the aim of anything called wisdom. Ultimately, for all its changes of perspective and intent, sapiential literature is dominated by the one idea—the permanent value of the human endeavour.

What Wisdom Achieves.

The one who is at home in the created world, and with creation's God, will live a fulfilled person. He will be *wise*, *hakam*—that is, co-ordinated and in control of life to the extent that it is possible to be.

This is the end product of the wisdom project.

If one wanted a word-characterization of the sage—he is *alert*. Morally and intellectually, such a one is in control of the task of living and coping with life; and there is always something of the "contestant" about him: he does not facilely accept, he questions; and is always prepared to apply the guideline of experience to any proposition:

> The simple believes everything,
> but the prudent looks where he is going.
>
> (Prov 14:15)

The wise is never credulous: he does not believe everything he hears, no matter how trustworthy the teacher. And he is unwilling to be dogmatic; in every circumstance the sage maintains a healthy sense of balance—and of humour:

> The way of a fool is right in his own eyes,
> but a wise man listens to advice.
>
> (Prov 12:15)

> The sluggard buries his hand in the dish,
> and will not even bring it back to his mouth.
>
> (Prov 19:24)

It is clear that the possession of wisdom is distinguished by a particular cast of mind and this is perhaps most clearly seen in what the wise most definitely deprecate: shoddy, slack thinking (Qoh 10:12–15); gossip, free-talking, indiscipline of mind or tongue (Prov 13:3). To these one can add the boor and the philistine, with whom society is replete. In other words, "wise" designates the truly human person, of intellectual and moral probity, of refined and cultured taste, capable of an adequate clarity of thought. One should be personally disciplined, and capable of bringing a disciplined mind to any life-situation, secular *or* religious.

Because of this fact, the "fool" one meets with frequently in the Wisdom literature is an important type character, for he is a conceptual "negative" of the "wise" person. In the first place, he is clearly not wise who thinks himself so—because this attitude makes one no longer open to new experiences and new suggestions, and this is the cardinal fault (Prov 26:12). Folly is seen as the disregard of what might readily be understood if one listened, and therefore bespeaks a lack of due mastery of what is, after all, a very human environment (Prov 10:14; Qoh 2:14). Indeed, folly leads inevitably to uncontrolled, and so inhuman, behaviour (Prov 12:16), and this leaves one vulnerable (Prov 14:17). "Folly" is thus more than merely a conceptualization of an intellectual weakness, more than a literary lay figure, as it were; it is a very human attitude, a disorder at the centre of a person's existence. The fool is contrary to the wise—he remains closed to the possibilities of human experience and is therefore incapable of learning. Such a one lives in the world as its prisoner, not its master.

At his best, the wise one is flexible, tolerant of ideas, never doctrinaire.

He is interested in facts and in ideas, of whatever provenance; and is therefore characterized by a refusal to be tied to assumptions—scientific or theological. Indeed in Proverbs alone we can trace a remarkable ethic of tolerance prescribed by the sages:

> do not cling to your own opinion, be
> open: 13:10; 30:32;
> and do not necessarily advocate it:
> 12:23; 29:20;
> never emphasize the faults of others:
> 10:12; 17:9;
> for knowledge worthy of the name is many-
> sided, and should be prized:
> 10:14; 17:27.

God indeed knows tolerance is a rare and fragile bloom, to be cherished.

One other requisite of the person who is wise is a cool head—which may be acquired by discipline; mental and emotional control. The hot-tempered person allows himself to be driven by passions he cannot control, and is therefore determined *by* his environment, rather than *dominant of it.* Lack of control makes one regrettably that less human:

> A man of quick temper acts foolishly,
> but a man of discretion is patient.
>
> He who is slow to anger has great understanding,
> but he who has a hasty temper exalts folly.
> (Prov 14:17, 29)
>
> He who restrains his words has knowledge,
> and he who has a cool spirit is a man of understanding.
> (Prov 17:27)

The world, however humanized, is a created world after all, and God remains part of the equation. God and world, however, are not identical. You must encounter one *in* the other. A truly human person achieves "life" when he or she encompasses the whole—the world of terrestrial experience and the world of God-experience. This is as close as one can come to a definition of the term "wise". Wisdom is both practical and theoretical; one who accepts the moral commitment of "walking in righteousness", and one who knows the right way (Prov 14:8). Respect for righteousness, or justice, was in one sense the end of the discipline of the sages, and was moral rather than forensic. It did of course call for justice in the sense of loyalty to an agreement (Prov 11:1) where cheating is an offence against God, and an offence against one's own self—one's word. However, the righteousness of the sage also called for active mercy: alms swiftly given (Prov 3:27; 21:26), respect for the ultimate judge, for he alone can judge equitably, with the benefit of all the evidence (Prov 20:22). Clearly, this is why mercy must be extended even to enemies (Prov 25:21). Indeed, with regard to love of enemies the sages went further than the *Tôrah*. For example, Sir 28:1–7 adds a dimension of common sinfulness, the possibility of earning forgiveness for one's own sins by recognition of the common factor of creation: "Forgive your neighbour the wrong he has done, and then your sins will be pardoned when you pray" (v. 2), "if he himself, being flesh, maintains wrath, who will make expiation for his sins?" (v. 5).

Wisdom, however, serves more than an ethical purpose: it is also geared to the acquisition of knowledge for its own sake, to a greater extent perhaps than allowed by extra-biblical literature. This is a significantly Israelite quality in wisdom, as manifested by the non-moral context of so many sayings. These have no moral or religious purpose, exhibiting merely the desire *to know* for the sheer love of knowledge,

> The heart has its own bitterness, and no
> stranger shares its joy.
>
> (Prov 14:10)

or wonder for the sheer fascination of the wonderful:

> Who has let the wild ass go free?
> Who has loosed the bonds of the swift ass,
> to whom I have given the steppe for his home,
> and the salt land for his dwelling place?
> He scorns the tumult of the city;
> he hears not the shouts of the driver.
>
> (Job 39:5–7)

Some Egyptian texts come close to this feeling of art for art's sake, but for the most part its proverbial literature has a moral aim. Mesopotamian sapiential texts have a marked religious or sacral aim.

The sapiential literature of the Old Testament is many-faceted, materially and functionally. We find writings where the content reflects a clear preoccupation with artistic self-expression—perhaps the first mark of the wisdom genre. Then there is the teaching preoccupation, giving its own didactic cast to so much of the literature. This type varies according to the particular needs of the society addressed, and the artistic concerns of the writer: personal cultivation, administration, religious education. It is as varied as the "life" it seeks to attain.

Who were "the Wise"?

The term most commonly used is *hakam*—in the singular or plural—the "wise". From the biblical evidence it is far from easy to say if this is meant to be descriptive of a general type, or if it actually designates a given group of people. Scholarly opinion is divided: some hold it refers to a teaching class, some an administrative or a social class.

To the prophets, they were a known and easily distinguishable group of people, eyed with no great favour by those stern upholders of the religious conscience. But the prophets were, for the most part, looking at one particular set of people in one particular situation—the court administrators and political advisers of the state (see below, p. 39). More primitive texts in the Old Testament apply the term "wise" to individuals, male and female, who by merit of age, experience or outstanding competence served as tribal advisers, and were accounted "wise" by their community. Later on, with the establishment of central government, we find the court secretary or counsellor assume the mantle of the wise. These were probably modelled on the Canaanite and Egyptian traditions of scribe and secretary, and were professions held in high honour. That such a world of scribes and secretaries was common to Israel also can be attested in many of the historical books. 2 Sam 8:16–17 describes David's royal entourage: "Joab the son of Zeruiah was over the army; and Jehoshaphat the son of Ahilud was recorder; and Zadok the son of Ahitub and Ahimelek the son of Abiathar were priests; and Seraiah was secretary." One finds the same sort of situation in 2 Sam 20:25 and 1 Chr 27:32.

As distinct from the Egyptian, Israelite wisdom is not rigidly tied to courts: it is often directed to government officials and social leaders, but it is more universal. Israelite wisdom expresses what is of concern to humanity, and does so artistically. Whatever its origin as found in the Old Testament it is self-consciously literary, and bespeaks a high standard of education. Jewish youth who were destined for the Civil Service had a very high standard to achieve—physical, moral and intellectual. Dan 1:3–5 gives us a free portrait from the Persian period:

> [3]Then the king commanded Ashpenaz, his chief eunuch, to bring some of the people of Israel, both of the royal family and of the nobility, [4]youths without blemish, handsome and skilful in all wisdom, endowed with knowledge, understanding learning and competent to serve in the king's palace, and to teach them the letters and language of the Chaldeans. [5]The king assigned them a daily portion of the rich food which the king ate, and of the wine which he drank. They were to be educated for three years, and at the end of that time they were to stand before the king.

This illustrates the educational system that lies behind the Old Testament Wisdom books. The first requirement, if one would begin to think of a career, was a literary training, an "arts degree", as it were. This left its mark on the tastes and inclinations of the students, even those who later on retired from, or lost their taste for office. Wis 7:17–22 gives some idea of the curriculum:

> [17] For it is he who gave me unerring
> knowledge of what exists,

to know the structure of the world
and the activity of the elements;
[18] the beginning and end and middle of
times,
the alternations of the solstices and
the changes of the seasons,
[19] the cycles of the year and the
constellations of the stars,
[20] the natures of animals and the
tempers of wild beasts,
the powers of spirits and the
reasonings of men,
the varieties of plants and the virtues
of roots;
[21] I learned both what is secret and
what is manifest,
[22] for wisdom, the fashioner of all
things, taught me.

A widely conceived course, indeed, embracing astrology, zoology, the occult, botany, psychology. Add to this what is found in 1 Sam 16:18—music, rhetoric and physical fitness—and one ends with a picture of the well-educated youth. Given maturity, one attains the scholar's rank: Sir 39:1–11, one whose calling it is to perceive truth, and give it a personal dedication, Sir 14:20–27.

The sapiential movement is marked by a supreme confidence that a literary and practical education, leavened by moral training, can produce balanced, incisive people, whole human beings. So in effect what one arrives at is an intellectual elite, intelligent and educated. This is the sort of person who can, in any society or age, be expected to possess practical worldly ability, a polished manner, be effective in life as in affairs, and cultivate a certain nobility of mind and action. Indeed, the Old Testament presents this as a portrait in 1 Kgs 4:29–34. While this is a description of Solomon, it is also a description of a particular *kind* of person and a particular society that could produce such: a society of cultivated people, given to letters and the arts, with a particular international cast of mind. Perhaps not a distinct "school" or "movement", but people with a distinct approach to life, one unlike that of the prophets.

A composite picture might be made: the "wise" were people who had, on the whole, a closer relationship to secular affairs—court, administration, education, letters—than to the Temple. The piety we find tends to be passionless, reserved; an accepted norm for personal life rather than religious enthusiasm or cultic devotion. It was not necessarily an organized movement, so much as a disparate professional or amateur avocation indulged by a certain type of person to whom affairs of the mind were important. It is difficult to find evidence of a professional teaching as such in the Old Testament—a manual for lawyers or scribes, as it were; what we do have is a form of literature polished to a degree of art. Thus *hakamîm*—the wise—is a broad term. Not just a school or a group who can be identified as such, but an inclination of mind, fruit of a literary and moral training. We are dealing with literary people, rather than with a merely professional group. If we can imagine a society of professional people, and leisured upper-middle class people with literary training or pretensions, who indulged in writing, or perhaps taught in a private family or in a public (and restricted) school for the élite; religion being to a great degree the substructure of their lives rather than a driving force; this is likely enough the ambient of the "wise". There is indeed sufficient biblical evidence for some kind of formal schooling for government and business officials. From extra-biblical literature we can at least arrive at a possibility for Israel—the existence of schools for the élite. Probably the first classes were shared by all, for the basic arts of reading and writing; then in higher grades the priestly candidates going on to strictly "seminary" training, and the secular students diversifying according to their projected careers. In the Babylonian system this was clearly so. There was a two-school system—the "house of tablets" for the uninitiated, and a higher ''house of wisdom'' for second level students. Such an arrangement in Israel could explain the various types of biblical literature—legal and sapiential.

CHAPTER 2
THE HISTORICAL CONTEXT

The Wisdom of Israel is not an isolated phenomenon, as is much of the rest of the Old Testament. Indeed, adequately to understand it, biblical wisdom literature must be viewed against the wider background of the major literatures of the Near East, for it is part of an international and intercultural tradition, comprising the literatures of Egypt, Mesopotamia and Israel. Thus a comparison of these cultures and the written works they produced illustrates the basic character of the sapiential tradition. Egypt and Mesopotamia evolved systems of instruction and speculation on life and on professional affairs and, like Israel, in both these cultures we find a common ground: instructions on proper behaviour, proverbs and precepts, a basic respect for scholarship and for academics, and a belief in an established order to which one had to conform. All of this was modified and reformed by the progress of history and the changes of life-style this brought.

Wisdom in the Near East

The literature of Egypt offers perhaps the closest parallels to Israel's sapiential literature, and the influence it had on this latter is noticeable. It is sufficient to mention the close similarity, perhaps even the dependance, of Prov 22:17–24:22 on the Egyptian *Instruction of Amen-em-ope.*

A closer look at the literature in question may supply a perspective. For reasons of clarity, scholars divide ancient Egyptian history into three periods. The relatively obscure Old Kingdom, beginning about 2686 B.C., was brought to an end by a political crisis some four hundred years later that left the land divided. This was followed by the Middle Kingdom, a period of intellectual growth that lasted until the Hyksos invasion (asiatics from the East) about 1800 B.C. With their eventual expulsion in the first quarter of the sixteenth century began the New Kingdom (circa 1570–1200), politically and culturally the high point of the Egyptian tradition. Thus, apart from two interludes of turmoil, the literature had a long flowering.

From the Biblical point of view, one of the most important forms of Egyptian literature was the "instruction". The instruction genre, from the Egyptian word *sboyet,* meaning "instruction", normally takes the form of an address by a sage to a pupil (or child) or a ruler. They contain both discourses on worldly wisdom and sagacity, and more specialist advice on statecraft. The *Instruction of Ptah-hotep* (possibly from the third millenium) is essentially a school text-book, inculcating good manners, but also emphasising the need for eloquence if the pupil is to succeed in public life. The *Instruction of Duauf,* from about 1300 B.C., shows all the marks of schoolboy handling. Clearly used as a class exercise to extol the value of education, it was written and re-written by generations of schoolchildren, and indeed exists only in the form of class notes. Far more serious is the *Instruction for King Meri-ka-re,* also very old (third millenium, perhaps?), in which a king instructs his heir in politics, statecraft and piety:

> Be wise in speech [my son], that you may prevail,
> for an individual's power is in the tongue, and
> speech is mightier than fighting.

One thinks of the emphasis Proverbs places on the wise use of language (10:13; 15:2; 20:15).

These "instructions" bear witness to the essentially stable nature of a life intellectually centered on a political, social and religious establishment. There was little confrontation, few pressures. The dominant factor in the literature is the concept of *ma'at,* a divine cosmic order and the ultimate value to which both gods and mankind were responsible. Basically, this system represents totality, rightness, with overtones of regularity and order. This can be seen in both art and literature. A common device in Egyptian tomb-painting is a depiction of a personalized *ma'at,* goddess of truth, who weighs the hearts of suppliants against the feather of "rightness". This idea is seen also in literature. For example, the obligations imposed on *Vizier Rek-mi-re* on his installation have regard to preserving *ma'at* in the land. The *Instruction of Ptah-hotep* shares this preoccupation. In the moral sense *ma'at* stood for an order of justice and of "truth", to which human life had to conform. In later writings this even extends to a mutual relationship between mankind and the environment. This can be inferred from the *Prayer of One Persecuted,* and several other "prayers" from the New Kingdom period. This cosmic rule or pattern became more anthropocentric in the later literature; new generations began to question the accepted traditions of the elders, as we find in the so-called *Wisdom of Ani.* This imitative piece of writing from the New Kingdom is a pastiche on the whole Instruction genre that reflects the point of view of a new generation with its own problems. It is a semi-humorous sketch on the solemnity and portentiousness of the old books of wisdom. Here a father instructs his son on the virtues of an ordered way of life, and the son's answer reflects something of the natural scepticism of youth towards such parental wisdom:

> The scribe Khenshotep answered his father Ani. "Ah, would that I were as good as you . . . in that case I would indeed act in accordance with your teaching!

> [But] *you* are a man of lofty desires, and all your words are well-chosen''.

The sarcasm is not far to seek. To such writers the discipline of Wisdom served to prepare one for life by showing the implications of the cosmic order and applying it to the human situation—and they were well aware of the fact that this situation was mutable. The ''wise'' were the transmitters of *ma'at* to *every* age. Other sapiential writings of the Instruction genre are the *Instruction of King Amen-em-het* and the *Instruction for Kagemni.*

Besides the purely instruction literature we find many school texts: model letters for aspiring writers; greetings to teachers and superiors; pedagogical exhortations to pupils, including one dealing with that fatal combination—beer and leisure:

> I am told you foresake study and apply yourself to pleasure instead. You wander from street to street, where it smells of beer . . . a dangerous companion.

This is the *Papyrus Anastasi,* and speaks from the point of view of the New Kingdom, but it might just as well be from the *Book of Proverbs* (20:1), the Paris schools of the Middle Ages, or any Polytechnic of the twentieth century. Also represented in the Egyptian tradition are love songs that remind one of the biblical *Canticle,* such as the allusively delicate song of *The Maiden in the Meadow,* and the *Trees in the Garden* with its emphatic sensuality:

> I was brought . . . as plunder for the beloved. She has set me in her orchard . . . and I set myself to drink. I am found for pleasure.

It is almost as if the incomplete form in which the song was transmitted itself moves the heart. A totally different kind of literature is the *Onomasticon,* or word list. This is a catalogue of names of things, places or persons which served as an aid to memory for pupils, and also as an effort at controlling the varied data of experience with a view to mastery of the human environment. An extended form of this may be found in the listing of creatures in Job 39—41, but its essential function is underlined by the opening words of the *List of Amen-ope* (New Kingdom): "The teaching about all that is".

More profound is the "Religious Complaint", which probes the mystery of human existence. Such is *A Man's Dispute with his Soul,* and the *Complaint of the Peasant,* both of which have been compared to Job and Qoheleth.

Mesopotamia, the "land between the rivers", presents a different picture, since it is widely accepted that the term "Wisdom" applies less here than it does in Egypt or Israel. Because of its different historical and social ambient, Mesopotamian literature exhibits much more internal tension. Socially and politically unstable, indeed often no more than a patchwork of city-states, it is much more a cultural melting-pot than Egypt—a mixture of Sumerian and Semitic. Here in the land between the rivers one finds a changing human and political scene that resulted in a more open questioning in literature of the relationship between the divine and the human. This literature also centred on a cosmic order—ME—a divine order in created things, though quite often the will of the gods is perceived as arbitrary and irrational.

The range of this literature parallels the international concern for meaning and life. The *Poem of the Righteous Sufferer* is an observation on world order, and *Man and his God* is a Job-like lament. Proverbs and fables abound in this tradition, as do popular sayings with the same earthy humour one finds in every folk-literature: the mouse who escaped from the mongoose, only to end up in the snake's den is a parable that needs no interpretation. The disintegration in this tradition is more sharp and obvious than in Egypt. The "dogma" of retribution that resulted from an over-extended application of ME breaks down more obviously in the later literature.

In many ways Israel combines a little of both these traditions. At first representing a stable situation, Old Testament Wisdom rapidly becomes more broken. While the influence of Egyptian literature is more evident in the older strata of biblical Wisdom, later texts manifest more affinities to Mesopotamia. The problem of retribution seems more central in these than in Egypt, where belief in an afterlife offered a solution. To both the Mesopotamian and Israelite death is the end of human existence, and any imbalance between human activity and its consequences had to be justified at the level of earthly life.

Israel's Wisdom was more international than any other part of the biblical tradition. However, while Israel honoured, and accepted, ideas from other sources, she always digested them and used them to best effect within her own theological categories. One aspect of this is seen in the way that the secular dimension common to Near Eastern writing is leavened every so often by a deeper consideration: the problem of theodicy, and of a just God. In Mesopotamia the *Dialogue of Pessimism* and the *Babylonian Theodicy* explore the traditional concept of an ordered universe in which equity is not only the rule but is also perceivable. In Israel, *Job, Qoheleth* and the *Dialogue of Agur and a Believer* (Prov 30:1–9) reflect the same preoccupation. Because of its belief in life after death Egypt lacks writing with the same bite.

Given this international background, it is not surprising that when Israel developed a theology of man and his world she did so in a very intellectually sophisticated setting, and took into account a rich legacy of a wisdom without frontiers, doing so quite self-consciously, as evidenced by 1 Kgs 4:29–34:

> [29]And God gave Solomon wisdom and understanding beyond measure, and largeness of mind like the sand on the seashore, [30]so that Solomon's wisdom surpassed the wisdom of all the people of the east, and all the wisdom of Egypt. [31]For he was wiser than all other men, wiser

> than Ethan the Ezrahite, and Heman, Calcol, and Darda, the sons of Mahol; and his fame was in all the nations round about. [32]He also uttered three thousand proverbs; and his songs were a thousand and five. [33]He spoke of trees, from the cedar that is in Lebanon to the hyssop that grows out of the wall; he spoke also of beasts, and of birds, and of reptiles, and of fish. [34]And men came from all peoples to hear the wisdom of Solomon, and from all the kings of the earth, who had heard of his wisdom.

Popular, and secular, wisdom was all right in its way; but the God-experience and the association of Yahweh and the world-order had to modify the foreign concepts, and added its own perception of God and his personal control of the Cosmos. In this way there evolved a wisdom genre that had to answer to a wider, and more overtly religious, context and a concept of the limits of purely human wisdom. In Israel, the fact of one, transcendent God in place of a vague and anthropomorphic pantheon with rather eccentric gods led to a clarity of thought and a basic intellectual control not found in neighbouring literatures.

The Development of Wisdom in Israel

Wisdom as a human attribute is a capacity, innate or acquired, to interrogate experience and evolve theories that enable one to achieve human fulfillment. As such, it developed within the context of human evolution, of changing historical and social circumstances.

The roots from which it evolved may be found in an *oral tradition* that remains to us in scattered texts in the Old Testament, such as the collections of sayings in the early strata of the *Book of Proverbs.* When the redactor(s) put together the final version of their book (probably in the fifth century B.C.) they had available smaller collections of older material, such as that found in 10:1—22:16 (attributed to Solomon, see below, p. 167) and 25:1—29:27, which were seemingly collected around the eighth century and probably existed in more or less the same form earlier. They are the embodiment of common experience expressed in general terms, sometimes using piety to intensify the application. The primitive wisdom found here gradually became ordered to a diversity of practical ends—farming, commerce, rural and urban life. From this it was but a short step to the ordering of common knowledge, and the common tradition of folk-wisdom shared by all on the basis of life-experience, to educational and political ends—how to rule, how to co-ordinate the elements of society (compare Prov 10:4–5 and 23:1–10).

Wisdom builds on nature, and as Israel evolved there were different kinds of needs to be met. Education for life began in the home, if we are to take Proverbs seriously:

> The rod and reproof give wisdom,
> but a child left to himself brings shame to his mother.

This is 29:15, but many other texts suggest the same thing—10:1 and 13:1 for example. Beyond this, a priestly caste called for its own instructions; and schools for scribes and administrators must also have been established, as also for Temple servants and the well-to-do. So it may be presumed that each had its own kind of wisdom. Precisely what form this took can only be inferred from such texts as Sir 39:1–4:

> On the other hand he who devotes himself to the study of the law of the Most High will seek out the wisdom of all the ancients, and will be concerned with prophecies. He will preserve the discourse of notable men and penetrate the subtleties of parables. He will seek out the hidden meanings of proverbs and be at home with the obscurities of parables. He will serve among great men, and appear among rulers. He will travel through the lands of foreign nations.

Certainly, schools of this kind were common in the Near East, and surely were known in Israel.

Indeed, when Israel became a monarchy she set up her institutions on the prevalent Egyptian-Canaanite model, with court officials, counsellors, a civil service and a standing army. This may have been a development repugnant to the older leaders such as Samuel, but it was inevitable, as indeed can be inferred from the warning in 1 Sam 8:11–18. As the monarchy grew, it became more independant of purely religious restraints, and the role of the "state secretary" (2 Sam 8:7) and the counsellor became more important. But as far as can be seen in the text of the Old Testament, the period of the monarchy from the ninth to the seventh centuries was also the period of the prophets, and the sages are seldom mentioned in their own right. It is therefore from the frequently prejudiced point of view of the prophets that one learns about the "wise".

The relationship between the two seems to be somewhat ambivalent. Certainly, the prophets criticized the state counsellors who served the monarchy for what to them was a secular orientation that they gave to politics and statecraft, and for their scepticism. But they also seem to have shared to some extent the same education. The Chronicler gives one an insight into the prophet/sage relationship:

> Therefore the Lord was angry with Amaziah and sent to him a prophet, who said to him, "Why have you resorted to the gods of a people, which did not deliver their own people from your hand?" But as he was speaking the king said to him, "Have we made you a royal counselor? Stop! Why should you be put to death?" So the prophet stopped, but said, "I know that God has determined to destroy you, because you have done this and have not listened to my counsel."
>
> (2 Chr 25:15–16)

This tension was quite overt in the eighth to seventh centuries. Hosea directly attacks the royal counsellors for encouraging the monarchy in its political pretensions (compare Hos 10:13 with Prov 22:8) and for palace intrigue:

> They made kings, but not through me.
> They set up princes, but without my knowledge.
> (Hos 8:4)

Isaiah in particular had harsh things to say of the royal advisers who seemed to think themselves the sole possessors of wisdom. Isa 31:1–3 reflects the complex situation:

> Woe to those who go down to Egypt for help
> and rely on horses,
> who trust in chariots because they are many
> and in horsemen because they are very strong,
> but do not look to the Holy One of Israel
> or consult the Lord!
> And yet he is wise and brings disaster,
> he does not call back his words,
> but will arise against the house of the evildoers,
> and against the helpers of those who work iniquity.
> The Egyptians are men, and not God; and their horses
> are flesh, and not spirit.
> When the Lord stretches out his hand,
> the helper will stumble, and he who is helped will fall,
> and they will all perish together.

Here the prophet attacks the wise men of Hezekiah for the advice they gave the king. As the prophet sees it, Yahweh is the source of wisdom, and Isaiah is very conscious of the fact that he himself stood before Yahweh (cf. Isa 6:1ff; 7:1ff).

A century later Jeremiah expressed his own reservations about the intellectuals who served the court:

> How can you say, "We are wise, and the law of the
> Lord is with us"?

But behold, the false pen of the scribes has made
it into a lie.
The wise men shall be put to shame, they shall be
dismayed and taken;
lo, they have rejected the word of the Lord,
and what wisdom is in them?

(Jer 8:8–9)

Yahweh is seen to be the one who pre-eminently exercises wisdom. One can see that already in his time (seventh century) the sages had an established place in society, and especially in the public eye (Jer 18:18). This seems to suggest a growing "establishment" aura about the sage, a situation indeed reflected in Prov 25:1, and the "men of Hezekiah king of Judah". Jeremiah is more even-handed than his predecessors in prophecy, for he decries all three establishment figures—prophet and priest as well as sage:

> Then they said, "Come, let us make plots against Jeremiah, for the law shall not perish from the priest, nor counsel from the wise, nor the word from the prophet. Come, let us smite him with the tongue, and let us not heed any of his words."
>
> (Jer 18:18)

It would be a mistake to accept the black-and-white judgement of the prophets at face value. The "wise" of Israel were long the custodians of a system of education and learning that influenced even the prophets. It is only when they dabbled in politics that the prophets turned against the sages, to whom many of them must have owed their education. The style of writing that one finds, especially in Hosea and Jeremiah, reflects the wisdom training: the rhetoric of Jer 13:22–23 for example, and the sapiential postscript of Hos 14:9 with its similarity to Prov 4:7–11. Traditionally, the sages had served the monarchy in the field of education, statecraft and in what was clearly an advisory capacity in government. From the evidence of the reign of Hezekiah they were also literary people, editors and writers.

By the fifth century the prophetic voice was stilled, the monarchy dissolved, and it is from this time on that the Wisdom Literature of the Old Testament, the written corpus we now have, evolved. It is thus, for the most part, Exilic or Post-exilic. Some of the collections in Proverbs are earlier, but the rest of the wisdom books were written between the fifth century (Job) and the first (Wisdom), and even Proverbs as it now stands was probably put together in the fifth century B.C. It is easy to see, then, how the theological point of departure for the sapiential books could well have been the Priestly tradition (also from the sixth-fifth centuries), with its emphasis on mankind created in the image of God (Gen 1:26; 5:1; 9:6). A comparison of the first Creation Narrative of Gen 1 and the Yahwistic second Narrative of Gen 2 shows how anthropocentric were the views of the Priestly authors (see above, p. 13). Indeed, the Book of Wisdom, which is quite late, bases its "new theology" of human immortality on the theological presuppositions of the Priestly tradition (see Wis 2:23). From this concept of God as creator, who commits the created world to the care and administration of humankind, follows logically man's quasi-autonomy in the continuing creation of the world. This relationship between God, humanity and world becomes very easily more than a moral principle: it becomes an intellectual principle and the basis of a theology of human responsibility and religious individualism. Here in all probability one finds the basic thrust of all the writings that come under the wisdom label, from the late redaction of Proverbs to Wisdom of Solomon. Since God is still creator, there is a decidedly universalist tinge to morality.

There is evident a certain dichotomy: while the sapiential tradition is as old as Canaan, the literature as such is late—due to the fact that (one hopes) thinking precedes writing. From the inarticulate wisdom of the craftsman to the sophisticated wisdom of the philosopher is a long, many-faceted perspective, marked by many stages and manifestations: wisdom and the art of coping with nature; the statesman and his craft; the world of the academic and the literary gentlefolk.

a) WISDOM AND THE ART OF COPING WITH NATURE.

There is no question of trying to trace the origins, as such, of wisdom—who can trace the origins of a people's folklore?—for these are as varied as is the human response to its environment. Mankind always learned from its environment: how to read the signs of weather and harvest; when to plant and reap; how to build; how to watch the world round about and actually plan ahead to achieve, or indeed forestall, a consequence. This is *hokma,* wisdom in its most fundamental form—the art of coping with life. One learns from one's milieu. At some stage the community or the group assimilates the art of survival, augments it, passes it on. When it is put into polished form it becomes popular wisdom:

> A slack hand causes poverty,
> but the hand of the diligent makes rich.
> One who gathers in summer is prudent,
> but one who sleeps in harvest brings shame.
>
> (Prov 10:4–5)

> Where there is no guidance, a people falls;
> but in an abundance of counsellors there is safety.
>
> (Prov 11:14)

> Better is a dry morsel with quiet
> than a house full of feasting with strife.
>
> (Prov 17:1)

This is particularly true when the perceptive intelligence makes the leap of analogy and one creates a true proverb:

> Like a bird that strays from its nest,
> is a man who strays from his home.
>
> (Prov 27:8)

There are many such wisdom characteristics to be found in the earliest strata of the Old Testament, and evidence that a truly "wisdom" genre existed from very early on—simple conclusions drawn from experience and transformed by the alchemy of the writer's art into a maxim or proverb. Popular wisdom, of field or town, is clearly based on an oral tradition. Whatever one may say about the overtly *religious* aspect of wisdom, the dynamic existed as long as the language did. The earliest type of sapiential literature we can distinguish, Old Wisdom, clearly shows its folk origins. Folk wisdom of a human cast, pertaining to *people* rather than to tribe or race, agrarian or urban, professional or artistic—it consists of norms for a good life, personal success, stability of the social order, shrewd observation. Even here at its most primitive level there is the idea of an underlying "order of things." This was correlated to observation: a certain kind of action normally resulted in a certain consequence; good or bad action generally led to a foreseeable end. Thus early proverbs and maxims contain the natural sanctions of human actions and their fruit; the sanctions of society itself; or for the more religious, reward or punishment meted out by the divinity. Local sages, elders of tribe or clan, functioned at this level, becoming repositories of the cumulative experience of the people. The Hebrew saw himself as very much involved in his own world and related to it. His ongoing activity of coping with life was in fact a process that made creation open to him and flexible towards him—it could serve him or dominate him, depending on his own attitude and his own intelligence.

> A stone will come back upon him who starts it rolling
>
> (Prov 26:27b)

This reflects the natural relationship between humanity and its environment, and the balance that was perceived between act and consequence, for good or for bad.

b) THE STATESMAN AND HIS CRAFT.

The Old Testament provides ample evidence that sapiential literature became formalized under David, and flourished within the royal administration of Solomon. The historical books that reflect this period make frequent mention of the probable precursors of the movement. 2 Sam 14 records an incident that took place during the early days of the monarchy under David, where a "wise woman of Tekoa" acts a decidedly wisdom role at the instigation of Joab—and indeed the "parable" she has recourse to is sapiential in form and style. In 2 Sam 20 we find another "wise woman," the time of Abel of Bethmaacah, whose political, or at least practical, sagacity saved the town. These two episodes feature ladies of ability, who were in all probability close to the popular wisdom of village life, elders with a weight of experience. The same text records the secretaries of the King, and 1 Chr 27 refers to the "court secretaries." These references to wise men and women, amateurs and professional secretaries, supply the link between popular and administrative wisdom. Under Solomon this latter must have flourished immensely. The "character-portrait" of Solomon himself as "author" of proverbs and wisdom-poems adds weight to this, as do the frequent references to his secretary with an Egyptian name (1 Kgs 4). This whole picture of court life bears the colouring of international wisdom—a court on the Egyptian model, a wise king-author, a "secretary" who is clearly political—a secretary of state in effect. A group of professional men-of-affairs and amateur litterateurs who composed literary proverbs and sayings, "spoke of trees . . . of beasts and birds, reptiles and fish," and "men come from all people" of the earth to share in this. Clearly an international movement, even without the obvious allusion to the Egyptian onomasticon genre.

In fact, the re-organization of Israel, around the 10th century B.C., resulted in the establishment of a monarchic administration modelled on local patterns, especially the Canaanite-Egyptian style. It became obvious that there was a need to apply wisdom to government, and indeed to teach the technique of government to aspiring officials and administrators, and the models on which they worked were already established in the older, and more stable monarchies. The king, as is the way with hereditary rulers, might or might not be efficient—the Civil Service had to be. So the predominance given to the literate, scribal secretary, and the fact that from the very early days of the royal court of Judah we know from the record the names of so many of the secretaries, makes it clear that here we are dealing with a society in which literacy was the art of a privileged class, and for such practitioners no post was beyond expectation.

c) WRITERS AND STATESMEN.

It is equally clear that such a society must have caused the literary caste to flourish; they had the education, the taste and the leisure. The court official relied on wisdom instruction, and the ideal of the public servant was always held up before him: well-educated, a convincing speaker who was capable of discreet silence, a knowledge of languages and professional expertise. We need look no further afield than the description of four young, promising officials that we saw in Dan 1:3–5 (p. 20 above), and the finished product as described by Sir 44:3–6:

> [3]There were those who ruled in
> their kingdoms,
> and were men renowned for
> their power,
> giving counsel by their
> understanding,
> and proclaiming prophecies;

[4]leaders of the people in their
deliberations
and in understanding of learning
for the people,
wise in their words of instruction;
[5]those who composed musical tunes,
and set forth verses in writing;
[6]rich men furnished with resources,
living peaceably in their
habitations—

Thus evolved the ideal of the cultured person, the whole person, well versed in self-discipline and in a variety of human arts. This is clearly the significance of *mûsar,* the "discipline" so favoured by the teachers, and so varied in its usage from Proverbs to Sirach. Such an educational preoccupation must have resulted in the growth of a cultivated class, and evidence that such existed in the biblical world may be found in the fact that education was very much an education in the liberal arts, and not merely in administration. One notes the artistic care taken over the formulation of simple proverbs such as Prov 14:13 and 16:1, and such elaborate artistry as Canticle of Canticles and Qoheleth. It is in this context that Solomon is seen as the "pattern of letters" and of the sapiential tradition. Whatever his actual contribution, and this is lost in the mists of obscurity, he established the social circumstances in which the career of letters became possible, and even honourable. It can be no cause for wonder that many of the more polished literary works in the wisdom corpus are artificially attributed to him.

The age of Solomon paved the way for a new use of old sapiential forms, and a more intellectual perception of the world, one that to a great degree prescinded from the religious. People now looked at the variety of human experience and sought to formulate it in an artistic way. This attitude fits an educated society. Faced with problems of international politics or private conduct, this class of person tended to decide for itself, without referring to oracles, occult *or* divine. In affairs of state a recourse to divine revelation might prove to be of little use, might even be obscure or incomplete. Far better to rely on one's God-given faculties. This is not to suggest that wisdom was at this stage irreligious. Rather was it para-religious. Faith in Yahweh there certainly was in the sophisticated court of Solomon, but religion had to meet the secular and form one world with it—and it was a new perception of things.

So "court" wisdom and "court" morality becomes more general, touching the ordinary life of individuals. There is no question of atheism or agnosticism—such an attitude was unthinkable. Rather was it a realistic, success-oriented, practical concern for the human world, impregnated to varying degrees with the spirit of Old Testament piety.

Yet to some extent the dichotomy was there, even if it remained implicit and no more. In the various strata of the tradition one can distinguish from the professional "teachers of state functionaries" and people of culture another type of sapiential writer: more concerned with morality, little preoccupied with affairs of state; addressing themselves to kings, rulers and society, it may be, but more committed to theology and its peculiar tensions.

The dichotomy, though real, must not be overemphasized. Purely Yahwist sources often indeed come out strongly against "political wisdom," as we know from some of the prophetic diatribes. But the preoccupation of such writers was monolithic, and not totally unprejudiced. The prophets as a class were never in danger of being accused of tolerance or broadmindedness. They had the sharply focused vision of extremists. In their view, the ruler was to defend covenant faith, administer justice (indeed, not far from the *teaching* of Proverbs, though alien to its *style*). In the realm of international politics, where the exigencies of politics demand a human expedience and an attention to the advice of counsellors of state and other wise men, the prophets were inflexible advocates of a different wisdom. Both contestator and civil servant sought the same thing, but had a different perspective. On the biblical evidence it is clear that in the 8th and 7th centuries the prophets frequently attacked the "wise", the statesmen who, to them, seemed to stand for religious compromise—but it is interesting to note that they do so in a language common to both, and they often seem to have shared the same educational background, before "specializing", as it were: for example, one notes the "proverb" style of Hos 4:11 (cf. Prov 20:1), 4:14 (cf 10:8; 10) and 8:7 (cf. 1:27; 11:27). There is also the rather "literary" reflection on nature we find in Isa 1:3 and the wisdom parable of Isa 28:23–29—good enough to appeal to the most exigent scribal teacher. Jeremiah's appeal to common experience (8:4–5; 18:13–17) is text-book wisdom. Furthermore, one thinks of Isa 3:10–15 and Jer 17:5–18 which state the concept of "retribution" in clinical terms; Jer 17:9–18 with its echoes of Prov 16:2; 21:2; 24:12 etc., and the proverbial cast of Amos 3:3–8.

Given the difference of point of view, sages and prophets are both purely Israelite, and they share a common belief and a common aim. The prophet, as always in human affairs, dreams of an ideal; it is the statesman's lot to find the practical expedient.

The Later Theological Preoccupation

While it is clear that the writers of the sapiential tradition had no interest in founding their point of view, or their teaching, on the Sinaic experience or the Covenant engagement in history—revelation as such played little part for them—they still lived within the Israelite tradition, and however secular their concerns, God was still involved in the world they encountered. They still spoke of Yahweh as arbiter of life, justice and morality. This can be seen in an early book like Proverbs, and a later work such as Sirach.

> The plans of the mind belong to man,
> but the answer of the tongue is from the Lord.

All the ways of a man are pure in his own eyes,
but the Lord weighs the spirit.
Commit your work to the Lord,
and your plans will be established.

(Prov 16:1–3)

This short section from one of the earlier collections of Proverbs reflects both the human initiative and the divine involvement. In spite of "the plans of the mind" God remains the directing agency in the affairs of individuals, just as he directs the moral order, as can be seen in the following verses:

The Lord has made everything for its purpose,
even the wicked for the day of trouble.
Every one who is arrogant is an abomination to the Lord;
be assured, he will not go unpunished.
By loyalty and faithfulness iniquity is atoned for,
and by the fear of the Lord a man avoids evil.

(Prov 16:4–6)

A much later author, *Sirach,* can express similar sentiments:

Do not ridicule a man who is bitter in soul,
for there is one who abases and exalts.

(Sir 7:11)

A similar idea is found in Sir 1:1–10 and Sir 24.

The central experience of God for the Old Testament was the experience of Sinai and the God of Creation. Clearly, for the prophets the creative and redemptive power of Yahweh is the motive for obedience. The sages, on the other hand, expressed little or no interest in this aspect of biblical tradition. They wished to procure "life", and God is part of that equation. Wisdom was not interested in the phenomenon of saving history, and this fact gives it a sharper, more actual, theological dimension. In intellectual circles faith had to justify itself more rigorously

—a growing independance from the traditions made this necessary. Freed from the literary mould of the creation-redemption tradition, both creation and world could be viewed from the empirical point of view—creation, not *as act,* but as experienced *fact,* becomes the focus of theology.

For instance, Deuteronomy is a book of religious renewal centered on the actuality of the Covenant and the abiding value of the Sinai experience. Deut 30:15 offers "life", but its perspective is markedly different to that of Proverbs, which also offers life.

> See, I have set before you this day life and good, death and evil. If you obey the commandments of the Lord your God which I command you this day, by loving the Lord your God, by walking in his ways, and by keeping his commandments and his statutes and his ordinances, then you shall live and multiply . . .
>
> (Deut 30:15–16)

Here the invitation to live is based on *Tôrah* religion, whereas in Prov 1—9 the invitation is based on practical experience of the world:

> Happy is the man who finds wisdom,
> and the man who gets understanding,
> for the gain from it is better than gain from silver
> and its profit better than gold.
> She is more precious than jewels,
> and nothing you desire can compare with her.
> Long life is in her right hand;
> in her left hand are riches and honour.
>
> (Prov 3:13–16)

Sirach is something of an exception, with its emphasis on *Tôrah* religion, but even here there is a practical note that comes from experience of life as it presents itself: social relations in daily life (8:1–9), marital affairs (9:1–9), and the art of statecraft (10:1–8).

Emphasis on the everyday, secular world and the affairs of mankind is the predominant wisdom attitude, but it acknowledges that this world, and its affairs, is ruled by God, and even though this tends not to obtrude, the very fact of God's involvement implies that moral decisions are as necessary as practical expedience.

Certainly, one of the factors that distinguished Israel's type of Wisdom was this integration of a strongly committed intellectuality with a specific concept of God that came from outside the tradition. Two of the most obvious examples are, of course, Job and Qoheleth. The very backbone of the Jobian drama lies in the polemic between Job and his three friends, who stand for the traditional view of God and world. To Job, God is cruel, unjust and arbitrary in his dealings with his creation—a view that has no origins in the tradition represented by Bildad the Shuhite:

> Behold, God will not reject a blameless man,
> nor take the hand of evildoers.
>
> (Job 8:20)

This is the voice of traditional faith, but Job has no such view:

> He crushes me with a tempest, and multiplies my
> wounds without cause . . .
> It is all one; therefore I say,
> he destroys both the blameless and the wicked.
>
> (Job 9:17,22)

His view is based on experience of life, not on the religious heritage. Even Eliphaz, the most gentle of traditional theologians, defends the dogma of a just God by an appeal to an almost prophetic source of inspiration:

> Now a word was brought to me stealthily,
> my ear received the whisper of it.

Amid thoughts from visions of the night,
when deep sleep falls on men . . . .
A form was before my eyes;
there was silence, then I heard a voice:
"Can mortal man be righteous before God?
Can a man be pure before his Maker?"
(Job 4:12–17)

But once again Job can only appeal to experience and reason:

God gives me up to the ungodly, and casts me into
the hands of the wicked.
I was at ease, and he broke me asunder; he seized me
by the neck and dashed me to pieces;
he set me up as his target, his archers surround me.
He slashes open my kidneys, and does not spare.
(Job 16:11–13)

A less emotional statement along the same lines is the longer argument in Qoh 7:23—9:12, dealing with human existence, the refutation of the traditional doctrine of the divine order in the world, and the uncertainty of man's destiny. The same point of view invades even the sapiential psalms, as Ps 73(72) and 37(36) bear witness. This intellectual orientation inevitably led to a very distinctive theology—the integration of the intellectual life with the life of faith.

Because of the unique element of revelation, real even when not explicit, the wise of Israel had to direct their daily lives according to two important norms: principles arising from human reason and intelligence, and principles derived from revelation. Naturally enough, this sometimes resulted in two types of ethic existing uncomfortably side by side: observance based on natural law (a standard of conduct in accordance with human dignity and experience), as in Prov 22:24–29; and observance based on the reality of Yahweh, as in Prov 22:22–23. More often, the two are integrated in a remarkably rich synthesis.

Justice is based, not on *Tôrah* legislation, or the concept of a shared experience of liberation, but on our common nature as creatures: see for example Prov 17:15 and 19:17. In 14:31 the religious dimension is indeed touched up—lightly, but even where this is not done at all the basic, unspoken, theological dimension remains: humanity with its created role in the world. The Wisdom of Israel is a unity—human orientated, creation based. In the later books, those reflecting the socio-religious tensions of a period of disintegration, the theological motif is dominant (especially in Job, Sirach and Wisdom), and wisdom becomes a divine call addressed to mankind, and in its own way allied to revelation. Indeed, it becomes personified (as in Prov 8, 9; Sir 24 and Wis 7—9), in some sense partaking of the divinity.

At no stage of its development, however, did the wisdom writers see reality as something uncontrolled by God, so in fact knowledge never functioned in absolute independance of faith. Even the doctrine of act-consequence, or "retribution" as it is frequently called, is far from being a universal law, or expressing universal causality. God can act even against the perceived laws of created things—a-rationally, as it were. The thesis of Old Testament Wisdom, frequently enshrined in the formula "fear of Yahweh is the beginning of wisdom," is that all human knowledge ultimately brings one back to the problem of God, his existence and his involvement. Therefore only an adequate relationship with God can put the human being in control of the environment, because only that can place him in the proper relationship with the phenomenon of experience.

The fact of God, and of the incalculable, contributed to the philosophical depth of the sapiential literature. It at once limited man—he became aware of his finite nature and the fact that he alone is not the measure of all things; and paradoxically carried him beyond any human goal he could envisage or attain by reason alone. However, there is another side to the later prominence of the God-dimension. The central intuition that God stands as ultimate arbiter of creation contains the seed of a major problem. If the world is amenable to reason and experience, what happens when the phenomena of experience no longer accord with theological tradition, when human reason comes into conflict with faith?

The Literature of Contestation.

The basic intellectual function of the wisdom writer was to establish a meaningful pattern in life, but it was equally likely that one might find it impossible to co-ordinate the world of experience and the tradition of faith. When the individual experience of life revealed a world that made no sense, then faith itself and its traditional mode of expression were endangered. The inherent weakness in a theology that postulated an "ordered system" was the simple fact that systematization tends to result in an oversimple generalization that becomes an intellectual soporific. This tends to close one's mind to new experiences that may not fit the traditional system. The phenomena of experience are seldom unambiguous—even for the most conventional wisdom there was always the incalculable. Because of this there must always be an adequate flexibility, an openness to new situations in which the divine order comes under attack, and the human intellect must be able to answer new questions in new circumstances.

Old Testament theology, like all systems of thought, met this crisis, and both prophet and sage turned to solve the problem, though in different ways. In all probability, the sapiential tradition reflects the most radical, and adequate, Old Testament response to the changed circumstances that faced post-exilic Israel.

The stages in which the problem developed are clear enough: the fundamental ethic of reward and punishment within a just order which formed the background of older theology gradually became more fundamentalist. As their response, the prophets purified the concept of Yahweh as administrator of the law of retribution by giving the idea a higher moral content, and by stressing the concept of individual responsibility. Wisdom approached the problem from the intellectual point of view and made it central. This process reflects the attitude of the times.

With the fall of the monarchy in 587 B.C. the sapiential movement cut its ties to king, court and politics. Instead, to some extent it *replaced* monarchy, an idea suggested by Isa 40:13–14:

> Who has directed the Spirit of the Lord,
> or as his counselor has instructed him?
> Whom did he consult for his enlightenment,
> and who taught him the path of justice,
> and taught him knowledge,
> and showed him the way of understanding?

Here royal or court wisdom seems to be attributed to God. Yahweh, it is said, used wisdom to create and govern the world. Initially, perhaps, this is the prophetic insight but after the Exile the Wisdom writers amplified the ideas of Deutero-Isaiah and Jeremiah. The view of Jer 10:12 is found in a more developed form, for example, in Prov 8:22–31.

> It is he who made the earth by his power,
> who established the world by his wisdom,
> and by his understanding stretched out the heavens.
> (Jer 10:12)

> The Lord created me at the beginning of his work,
> the first of his acts of old.
> Ages ago I was set up, at the first, before the beginning of the earth.
> When there were no depths I was brought forth,
> when there were no springs abounding with water . . .
> When he established the heavens, I was there,
> when he drew a circle on the face of the deep,

when he made firm the skies above,
when he established the fountains of the deep . . .
then I was beside him, like a master workman;
and I was daily his delight . . .
rejoicing in his inhabited world and delighting in
the sons of men.

(Prov 8:22–24, 27–28, 30–31)

It was time for change. The period from the seventh to the sixth centuries was one of crisis in Israel. The turmoil and instability of the last years of the monarchy shook the traditions of the faith, with the inevitable result that there arose a new generation with more "rational" and practical views. Israel became more vulnerable to outside values and secular ideas. Since such had always been congenial to the sapiential movement, this found itself more competent to cope than did the more cultic and prophetic movements.

In the first place, traditional theology was in question, and the wise had always liked questions. The older prophetic teaching was increasingly unacceptable to a generation made sceptical by the turmoil of history and the dissolution of political and social structures. Even the prophets themselves wryly reflect the predominant attitude of the "intelligensia" to their preaching. Zeph 1:12 presents the thesis—"Yahweh does neither good nor bad." A younger generation presumed that a god who allowed evil to flourish was at best aloof and uninvolved. Many of the psalms, such as Ps 14 (13) and Ps 53 (52), reflect this intellectual attitude by drawing attention to the "enemies" who "say in their hearts 'there is no God'." These enemies were now in part members of the people of God. Hab 1:2–4 takes up this idea, but by using a lament form shows a broadening of the attitude of disbelief in divine order, offering in evidence the triumph of evil over good, in this way presenting the individual problem as an intellectual universal. By the time Ezek 18:25–29 came to be written this had become an academic thesis.

The political and social situation reflected this crisis.

The courtiers and civil servants of the capital had always been somewhat feeble adherents of covenant faith; now as political winds changed they became more and more self-interested, looking to their own future and their own skin. Because of this a generation was coming into prominence, having little common ground with their elders (cf. Jer 31:29 and Ezek 18:2) even in religious belief. Individualism is often seen as the contribution of the prophets of the Exile, but in fact these do little more than reflect the spirit of the times, the radical religious scepticism that followed the collapse of the "theology of divine order" established by the tradition. And they were bitter indeed at finding themselves heirs to a situation they had not created. So, inevitably, some thinkers questioned the tradition, and sought a solution that was *intellectually* viable. Ezekiel reflects this critical attitude in chapters 14, 18 and 33. The Exile weakened the concept of Israel's solidarity as a covenant people, and brought to prominence the individual and his relationship to Yahweh. But this was now frequently a consciousness of isolation from the traditions of faith. This being so, it became a matter of each individual responding to his own existential situation.

This is clearly reflected in the sapiential literature, especially in Proverbs (chapter 30, as will be explained below, pp. 237ff), Job and Qoheleth. Rational appraisal of man's situation in the world confirms the one-to-one relationship as the only trustworthy basis either of religious faith or its alternative, rationalism. So the burning question faced by Wisdom's literature of contestation is this: given the actual human situation, is the individual capable of doing something, or is he a random leaf carried along on the stream of life? In the Wisdom literature of the Old Testament it is easy to trace the development of a theme, or better, two aspects of a problem. For some, a religious individuality was possible—a relationship to God, a personal search for meaning, a fear of divine punishment. But a later theological speculation emerges under the threat of changing times, and criticizes the notions of reward and responsibility and divine order, in both its personal and its collective aspects. In most of the older literature these rest easy bedfellows, with no apparent tension. But from the time of the Exile the inconsistencies between the tradition of the just being rewarded and the all too evident fact that they are not, the conflict between belief and experience, was seen and expressed.

Some of the older collections of maxims, found in Prov 10–22 and 25–29 reflect this. The reward foreseen for righteousness is "life", to which are attached the values that make this worth the name: prosperity, honour, reputation. This leads to a principle that if prosperity is a reward for merit, it is also a *sign* of merit and character, and calamity a sign of sin. This theory of retribution is Deuteronomic in tone (dating from the reign of the reforming king, Josiah, 640–609 B.C.), even as it is found in Proverbs and Sirach, and owes much to Egyptian thought. The harsh lines of contestation were often leavened with the acceptancc of mystery in life. Indeed, Wisdom even made progress in distinguishing between the ethical and the eudaemonistic by postulating a variety of theories allied to retribution: the expiatory value of suffering (Eliphaz' argument in Job 4–5); the solution of Ps 37 (36) of the consciousness of the presence and approval of God as its own reward; and ultimately of course the concept of a life with God beyond the grave, though this is limited to the last of the sapiential books, The Wisdom of Solomon. For the rest of the tradition death is the ultimate end of man, and the terrestrial is determinative. Otherwise, some external experience is necessary to confirm faith *as a religious attitude*—the Theophany of Job and Ps 73 (72). What is left is a scepticism tinged with a certain cool acceptance of theism as a postulate of the mind, as in Qoheleth.

Here we find the contribution of the Wisdom psalms. In these poems the procedure of the sages is applied to final theological concepts of faith and divine providence, Ps 73 (72); covenant ethics, Pss 15 (14) and 112 (111); and a personal piety that verges on the mystical (Ps 1). Even here, there is a determined effort to preserve their wisdom principles of looking at what happens to man in the world as part of the activity of a very personal God.

Biblical faith is an attitude of trust, a confidence in someone who has demonstrated his trustworthiness, so it partakes essentially of this personal dimension. Thus, as the opening up of one person to another it is trust rather than belief or intellectual assent to articles or tenets of a religion. So at this level a "vision of faith" does not involve a philosophical problem of "faith against reason." This occurs only when faith has become codified and propositional. Hence it is Later Wisdom that encounters the intellectual conflict of experience and faith—for faith had, by the Exile, become an immutable doctrine of God's order in the universe. The Book of Job is the classic example. Man's relationship to a world he did not create and cannot change, and to a God who defies reason in his treatment of his creature, is examined on the basis of the Wisdom principle of experience. Faith, grace, reason interplay. Typical of the genre, Yahweh as covenant God is not explicitly involved, but there can be no reasonable doubt that the covenant relationship between God and the righteous is the point at issue (cf. chapters 29–31). Experience has disproved the law of act and consequence, and the author makes no concession to a blind belief in traditional theology. As appears in the earlier wisdom strata, the sages were well aware of the fact that much in life, as it is experienced, is incalculable and God is free. Perhaps he has reasons unknown to mankind. But the main insight of Job, Qoheleth and Agur is that experience and reason leave little room for traditional faith (of act-consequence). A new answer had to be found, and to some extent the later syntheses contributed this.

The Later Syntheses.

There is evidence to suggest that schools founded in the post-exilic period contributed to a flourishing and a diversification of Wisdom. The Book of Sirach gives us fascinating glimpses of his own life and labours as a scribe; his academic training, discipline in study, travel and discussion—Sir 34:9–12; 39:1–5; 41:13–21. Besides these formal statements, we find a variety of collections of professorial and academic "lecture notes", particularly in Prov 1—9 and Qoheleth, as well as romantic fiction in the style of Tobias. All belong to the later flowering of the wisdom movement.

It is not so much that this later Wisdom was more religious, and older Wisdom more secular. Rather, in later Wisdom, the scope of the search became more narrowly focused, and this resulted in a more intense theological reflection. In the later syntheses there is little opposition between secularity and religion to be found. This is seen in the fact that the equation between "wisdom" as a human attribute and "fear of the Lord" is more obvious; wisdom becomes more clearly associated with *Tôrah* (especially in Prov 1—9 and Sir), and indeed is viewed more as a gift of God. And there is found a moralizing tendency, "justice" or righteousness is now measured against the scale of *God's* will rather than a human perception of order.

For later Wisdom the first principle of ethical teaching was "fear of the Lord," and here the connection with the deuteronomic tradition is maintained, though the thrust is changed. The deuteronomic principle was determined by the idea that "to be happy in the Lord" was the point of covenant observance. Now this becomes interiorized, the "happiness" of the righteous was seen as a present inner condition of soul, which reached its full flowering in the concept of *sumbiosin Theou* "living with God" as it developed in the Book of Wisdom. This is a new integration of humanism and religious commitment—wisdom now is "fear of the Lord," and fear of the Lord *is* wisdom, the vital dynamic of living a full life.

This also represents a development from the idea of retribution to the idea of virtue as its own reward. To live well guaranteed the most valuable of all gifts, familiarity with God. This more speculative idea never replaced the older concept, but rather expanded it and opened it out, standing side by side in the tradition with the living religious belief enshrined in the doctrine of act and consequence.

The later wisdom writers were representatives of a school that had a very comprehensive grasp of the theological tradition—possibly more so than that reached by any other group in Israel. They achieved a synthesis of creation/revelation not before reached. Beginning with the world, and the secular, they evolved a world-view that fuelled universal statements about the world and its mysteries and the broader concept of an all-embracing *truth*—for example, in Sir 24 and Wis 7—9 Wisdom has a cosmic scope. In its evolution the movement culminates in the concept of wisdom personified (cf. also Prov 8—9).

Indeed it is especially in the late flowering of Wisdom, in such books as Sirach and Wisdom of Solomon, that Israel's religion made a distinctive impact on traditional wisdom. The problem of theodicy is faced more squarely—from a totally new perspective; that of man as the image of God's eternity. In this way the new concept of immortality is developed, and all of this changes, and indeed deepens, the concept of faith itself. Especially here we have a smooth integration of secular and religious, each influencing the other.

In the post-exilic period represented especially by Sirach and Wisdom of Solomon, wisdom is applied to God: he is its possessor *par excellence,* it becomes a divine attribute. Indeed, this was to have a wide-reaching effect on the development of theology: one sees how wisdom thus becomes the way God presents himself to mankind to invite them to intimacy. It is particularly here, in the explicit joining of wisdom and faith, that we find the concept of God as originator of knowledge and wisdom. The short essay in Sir 6:18–37 shows this, beginning with the traditional idea of discipline and arriving at the concept of divine gift:

> My son, from your youth up choose instruction,
> and until you are old you will keep finding wisdom.

> Come to her like one who plows and sows,
> and wait for her good harvest . . .
> Reflect on the statutes of the Lord,
> and meditate at all times on his commandments.
> It is he who will give insight to your mind,
> and your desire for wisdom will be granted.
>
> (Sir 6:18–19, 37)

The Book of Wisdom is more explicit in speaking of the divine origin of wisdom, using philosophical terminology to describe her nature:

> For wisdom is more mobile than any motion;
> because of her pureness she pervades and penetrates
> all things.
> For she is a breath of the power of God,
> and a pure emanation of the glory of the Almighty;
> therefore nothing defiled gains entrance into her.
> For she is a reflection of eternal light,
> a spotless mirror of the working of God.
>
> (Wis 7:24–26)

The wisdom poem that one finds in *Baruch,* 3:9—4:4, presents wisdom as solely the gift of God. It cannot be achieved by human effort, for it comes only where the divinity chooses to bestow it—and he chooses Israel.

The gift of mind and intellect was not seen as just another gift, like prosperity or longevity. There was something theologically unusual about it. "Understanding" is not a characteristic *ex natura sua,* and is not given to everyone. Elihu gives a hint of this in the later addition to Job, in chapter 32:6–11. In some way the gift of wisdom parallels the gift of prophetic inspiration as a divine initiative (Job 4:12).

One further idea that emerges late in the development, due in part to the idea of wisdom personified, is the association of wisdom and God, to the extent that wisdom shares something of God's transcendence, therefore it can no longer be attained by human effort alone. Here, at the end of a long line of the development of the sapiential tradition, we see a modification, from the early principle of experience and human discipline to grace or gift, the result of religious practice. This insight is a result of the sages' growing theological preoccupation with God and his relationship to the world. He created the world by his wisdom [Ps 104 (103), Jer 10] and this probably lies behind the story of Solomon and his gift of wisdom (1 Kgs 3:4) which left an indelible mark on the wisdom writers.

CHAPTER 3.
GOODNESS OF LIFE: THE GOAL OF WISDOM.

The end which wisdom sought to achieve was clearly *holiness,* or in the wisdom perspective, "goodness of life." In sapiential literature this is a rich and profound concept of wholeness, more mature perhaps than the concept of holiness found elsewhere in the Old Testament.

By his very nature, man strives for the "good". This was experienced by Israel simply as a force that determined the shape of existence; something that arose from the experience of daily life as contributory to *shalôm,* the "peace" that is total human fulfillment. It is a dynamic, rather than merely a characteristic, and is creative of social conditions.

A person's behaviour was in some way connected organically with his environment, and was a constructive quality of good in that environment, or a destructive quality of bad; but the adjective is significant—it shows that the quality was seen as something creative, and therefore "goodness" was conceived of as a force that ensured man's act would be creative of, and not just protective of, true human and social *shalôm* (Prov 28:12).

The Good as Material Prosperity.

The first consequence of this way of thinking brought out by the sages was the belief that a person who embodies the "good", whose acts are good acts, is also prosperous and successful. He fulfills the claims made upon him by the community (Prov 11:10–11).

Most commonly, the term used for this quality in a person is "righteousness". The idea of "righteous", that is, the good and prosperous, is so nebulous when taken out of its context, and so well-balanced a mental image, that it is virtually impossible to translate. It is certainly difficult to communicate. Even the Hebrews themselves tended to lose sight of the real, inner, meaning of the concept, and as often as not ended up associating "rich" with "good", whereas the two are far more tenuously connected. "Righteous" is a daringly evocative concept, and the more pedestrian idea of rich/good is inadequate to communicate its full flavour. In the first place, righteousness (or in Hebrew, *sedaqâ*) is a relationship one has with God—an absolute, and never an approximate relationship. The wisdom project, the search after wholeness, dominates this literature when the sages appropriate righteousness to themselves as the fruit of wisdom. This is perhaps best seen in Proverbs, some wisdom psalms such as 73 (72), 1, and 119 (118), and the Wisdom of Solomon. The piety that we find depicted here is a deeply interior one, and is seen most clearly in the writing of the sages who evolved a surprisingly modern, psychological and affective understanding of the happiness that is nearness to God. For example, Ps 73 (72) presents an insight that is the fruit of a bitter intellectual and emotional struggle:

> [28]But for me it is good to be near
> God;
> I have made the Lord God my
> refuge,
> that I may tell of all thy works.
>
> (v. 28)

This is no more than one intense moment in what is a long evolution in the sages' perception of holiness.

Fundamentally, the sapiential conception of holiness is tied to a religious pattern of life in which material goods were realistically accepted, and were seen as blessings given to the one who was "good"—thus material prosperity was part of all that went to make up his goodness. Yet this was not purely materialistic. Even the poor man, it is recognized, can have honour and learning, and so can, in a manner of speaking, be termed wealthy or prosperous (Sir 10:30–31). One must be careful, therefore, in assessing the "rich is good" equation. Certainly, material prosperity is often involved, but not of necessity, and not alone. Indeed, one is often encouraged to "think success", but again the word "success" has wider connotations than the sense in which it is now taken. A pious integration of the person into an order of existence in which blessedness can be found is what is in question—but it is all bounded by the Hebrew categories of the material and the terrestrial; *this* life, concrete and singular. Added to this is the fact that *sedaqâ* (righteousness) is not a surface quality, and consequently is not always easily discernible. It must be *learned.* He who *is* good, *does* good and *produces* good. Material property does one good, as does a family, a friend, good repute. Without these you can scarcely *be* good, for things are not going well with you. What we have at this first and most basic level, then, is a concept of material and spiritual well-being. Thus the search for happiness and fulfillment is a natural human vocation, and when acquired both of these qualities constitute "life". And this is true, not just of Israel, but of mankind—it embraces all those who share the basic gift of human existence. In this way "wisdom" is clearly an art to be learned by all who are caught up in daily affairs—the art of choosing the right way, of knowing how to distinguish, in each situation of life, what is right, what is conducive to the "good".

The Social Dimension.

So, for example, Proverbs does not have a "moral theology" as such, or an ethics. It has instead a broad-based concept of "goodness". Righteousness is a relationship to reality, to the totality of what can be experienced, whether it be the controllable or the transcendent. So it is this reality that determines how one should act in a given situation: not a code of laws or commandments, not expediency, but a relationship to the society and the world in which God has placed one. Prov 16:27–30 exemplifies this attitude:

> A worthless man plots evil,
> and his speech is like a scorching fire.
> A perverse man spreads strife,
> and a whisperer separates close friends.
> A man of violence entices his neighbour,
> and leads him in a way that is not good.
> He who winks his eyes plans perverse things,
> he who compresses his lips brings evil to pass.

Indeed, the same terms of reference are used throughout, where social justice or communal life are in question (see for example, Prov 10:4–5, 15–16; 11:10–14; 14:34–35; 20:1–8). Prov 22:1–4 speaks of the "creational" value before God of each individual:

> A good name is to be chosen rather than great riches,
> and favour is better than silver or gold.
> The rich and the poor meet together;
> the Lord is the maker of them all.
> A prudent man sees danger and hides himself;
> but the simple go on, and suffer for it.
> The reward for humility and fear of the Lord
> is riches and honour and life.

Prov 22:9–10 is clearly orientated to the well-being of any given community:

> He who has a bountiful eye will be blessed,
> for he shares his bread with the poor.
> Drive out a scoffer, and strife will go out,
> and quarreling and abuse will cease.

So, and this is particularly true of Proverbs, morality is determined by a given community concept of man, and by its own traditions of the "right" and the "good". It might be called "situation ethics" if one remembers that a principle of divinely established creation is always presumed. What is important, therefore, is less the "how?" of one's actions than the "why?": is it in accord with created order or not? It is clear that the life-situation conceived of by much of the Wisdom literature is settled—that is, an established and determined community, either urban or rural. A world of rulers, administrators, workers, teachers. It is certainly not a world of crisis. There is indeed confrontation, but between what is clearly good and clearly bad, the ordinary citizen and the "corner-boy element", the disruptive force in the community (Prov 1:10–19). This sort of confrontation is not one of principle, not at the intellectual level. The rebels are no more than "silly fools," they have not enough intelligence to be doctrinaire. In fact, the term used in Proverbs is enlightening: a failure in "goodness" is not necessarily a *sin* (the term used being *pesha'*), but rather a lapse in the due relationship between people, or between the individual and God. The threefold distinction in Ps 1—righteous, sinner and *wicked*—is interesting.

The motivation for acting in a "good" way, as found for example in Proverbs and Sirach, is equally interesting. It almost always concerns stability in human relationships—if one hurts the community one is oneself hurt. To that extent we are dealing with a world-orientated ethic, based on a community's experience of the natural order and inherent natural laws. And since the individual, because of his or her created nature, always stands in a relationship, however unarticulated, with Yahweh, this ethic is in its own way an aspect of faith.

Goodness and Faith.

Because of its own particular apprehension of "the good", the sapiential writing makes an important contribution to the concept of *faith.* Religion is seldom presented here as a blind, or uncritical, obedience to a law or a commandment. Rather, the transcendent is *encountered* in all the finite relationships of life as the ultimate principle on which they are based. Through one's experience of these relationships, to people and things alike, one experiences God and responds to him and to his order. Faith is thus a response to the way things are, and not immediately a response to the transcendent. The genius of the sages is that their writings can frequently present a clearly secular world with secular values, and by this very fact enhance a theology of God and the world by underlining the tensions inherent in the world of the human, and the concomitant knowledge of God's unlimited influence over all the phenomena of experience. So "goodness" is a very definite perception of a close relationship to God and a harmonious relationship to the human environment. Life in common—for indeed in their perception man is social—is based on reciprocity, reliability and responsibility; an accord between the intentions of the mind and the actions "of the hand". If this accord fails, so does the very basis of human existence. Thus the great enemy of the good is not the bad, but the *lie,* the non-truth.

A lie—and the term is wider in its implications than non-semitic languages allow—is possible only where "truth" has already been established and perceived, and is directed against this existent truth. It is thus a breach of due relationship. From the *personal* point of view, the lie is, in the Old Testament perspective, an act of self treason, a betrayal of one's own selfhood. From the community point of view the lie is seen as a social evil, an injury done to a neighbour's sphere of being. "A truthful witness saves lives, but one who utters lies is a betrayer", according to Prov 14:25, and this is echoed in 14:5; 12:22; 19:22. With the later sapiential development, as the individual took the centre of the stage and his perception of *self* grew (his own self and that of the other), the lie is seen as an injury done to the structure of the human spirit. Sir 7:13 speaks of personal integrity: "refuse to utter any lie, for the habit of lying serves no good'', and the idea is found also in Sir 5:8–14. One's word must conform to the truth, because one's word is ultimately no less than the articulation of one's being.

Familiarity with God.

What decisively marks wisdom piety is the fact that God knows one, and one can know God. In this context the verb ''know'' (*yd'*) has a purely existential connotation. It is determined by human intercourse and not merely by perception. The life of the ''good'' or the ''wise'', effectively synonymous here, is so constructed that he can experience God in all the contexts of life, and each context is marked by this God-man contact.

The first glimpse we get of this is in Ps 73 (72), a wisdom psalm which deals with a personal crisis that is both intellectual and emotional. Here the *person* is involved in the problem of retribution, and of God's justice (or lack of it) in dealing with humanity. The concept of ''goodness'' as a very personal ''nearness to God'' that we find in vv. 23–24 is characteristic of the best of wisdom piety. Here the solution to the problem of alienation is a personal consciousness of the presence and approval of God. More, this proximity to God is perceived as the only due reward of piety, and piety's only goal.

But the wisdom writers go further than this in their exploration of ''the good''. The perception of God's nearness leads to a more intimate and evolved concept of ''delighting'' in the Lord. In Job 22:26 Eliphaz, honourable defender of traditional piety, describes the sage's ''religion of success'': ''then you will *delight yourself* in the Almighty''. Here the verb ''delight'' (*'anag*) used in the hitpael or reflexive form implies a joy that is sensual and intimate (it is used in this sense for example in Cant 7:7 and Mic 1:16) as well as religious. Here, and in Job 27:10, where the same term is used, we are dealing with a spiritual experience that is mystical in character. Ps 37 (36), also a wisdom psalm, takes up the same idea: "Take delight in the Lord, and he will give you the desires of your heart" (v 4). Here the material good is preserved alongside the purely spiritual as we see in the following verses in each text: Job 22:27–28 and especially Ps 37 (36):11, where it is said that "the meek shall . . . delight themselves in prosperity". Possibly the finest flowering of this truly wisdom concept of mystical union is found in Ps 1, the Wisdom psalm *par excellence.*

Ps 1 begins with a *statement of fact,* not a wish, not a prayer: "Happy is the one . . .", and it describes the state of one who chooses to walk in the way of goodness. He *is* happy, a truly fulfilled person. So the reader must ask: in what can this happiness, or goodness, consist? The deliberate antithetic parallel with which the psalm opens, a negative and a positive portrait, draws attention to v. 2, which is positive: his blessedness consists in the fact that "his *delight* is in the law of the Lord". Here the verb used is *hps,* "delight", with a significance similar to that found in Job and Ps 37 (36). It is an interesting concept. In normal circumstances it refers to the summit of human affection, that which exists between two people. Especially when followed by the preposition "in", as here, it is a subjective and spiritual attitude, with clearly affective overtones; a strongly felt *emotion* for God's will, and a quasi-sensual delight in conformity to this will.

These two characteristics occur in confessional form in Ps 119 (118), again a wisdom psalm. Here we are concerned more formally with the totality of the revelation of God's will, and yet what dominates the psalm is the idea of the total joy one finds in this revelation, which is a source of delight. All of one's striving after wisdom, or "insight", is directed to this very end which becomes the centre of one's emotional life, and the goal of one's striving. One finds that the most intimate expression of this human fulfillment occurs in such confessional, and therefore personal, forms, but they must not be seen in terms of a modern *apologia* (as von Rad points out). They stand as types of the perfect human being, and thus transcend human expression. They can therefore be expressed only existentially. Indeed, at this level of the expression of holiness, the sages become theological adventurers. Terms are used that intensify the experiential nature of the union, various perspectives are presented so as to form a composite picture. Thus the literary expression becomes pregnant with a sense of psychological as well as theological fulfillment.

The fulfillment that is experienced by the one who chooses wisdom over folly transcends ethics, transcends the moral values by which it is procured. Nor is it merely self-satisfaction for it goes far beyond self-consciousness. It is the result of an experience of intercourse with God—and there is a great deal of precision in the way Ps 1, in concluding, makes this clear: "God *is knowing* the way of the just". As elsewhere in the Hebrew bible, the use of the verb "to know" is significant. So is the deliberate contrast with the wicked—they fall to pieces and cease to be of any substantive importance: v. 6. Indeed, the same Hebrew verb ("perish, destroy") is used to a like effect in Prov 1:32 to describe the result of the fool's complacence.

The Wisdom of Solomon, with its concept of human immortality, is merely one logical step further. Such is the created nature of the human being that such a union with God, once attained, cannot be thought of as bounded by mortality. Such communion of life with God must partake of the divine nature itself, and therefore of the eternal.

CHAPTER 4.
KEY THEMES OF WISDOM LITERATURE.

A certain number of themes dominates the literature of the wise. Since most of the written corpus of this literature extends through five centuries (from Job in the fifth century to Wisdom in the first) there is some variation in significance and emphasis in the terms used, yet an overall unity may be perceived. As the sages and teachers sought to confront the multiplicity of human experience, and the concomitant experience of the divine, a natural synthesis evolved around certain key perceptions, and these occur at crucial points to focus experience and give some cohesion to the tradition.

The Fear of the Lord.

The concept of "fear" occurs frequently enough in the Wisdom literature to define the inner nature of wisdom, or knowledge. It plays a crucial role in the integration of secular and religious morality, and indeed, "fear of the Lord" is almost a formula of integration, since it is used to link the various aspects of wisdom. Its first basis is *knowledge,* and it is therefore closely associated with the educational process: "The fear of the Lord is the beginning of knowledge" is the editorial perception of Prov 1:7. At its first level it probably meant no more than the religious education of the Israelite, but gradually it became identified as the foundation of any true conscience, or the human consciousness of permanent value. Job 28:28 expresses the belief of the post-exilic sages, among whom wisdom was thought to be accessible to man and a principle of morality:

> And he said to man,
> "Behold, the fear of the Lord, that is wisdom;
> and to depart from evil is understanding."

Sir 1:11–20 exalts "fear" as something akin to a sense of religion, and v. 19 is particularly significant:

> He saw her and apportioned her;
> he rained down knowledge and discerning
>   comprehension,
> and he exalted the glory of those who held her fast.

Fear derives from an experience of God and an intimacy of association with him; one learns about him as one learns about any friend (Prov 3:32). Essentially, it is an offshoot of intimacy with the divine.

In its primary manifestation it is more intellectual than moral, *knowing* is anterior to *doing*. Fear, then, is a source of wisdom, a way of access to understanding and intelligence. It may be a gift of God that enlightens the human mind, but it is also an acquired quality. One can learn to *know* the true and the good. But the more broad-based knowledge is, the more secure a guide one finds in it, and there is no knowledge that does not ultimately cast the seeker back on the question of self-knowledge. What is mankind all about? What is human existence? Who are we? Without an awareness of these ramifications to life there is no "fear", for knowledge is too narrowly established. The use of the term in Proverbs is interesting.

It occurs fourteen times, and one finds on analysis that it is a broader statement about life and knowledge that is immediately obvious, for there lies under the surface of the concept an awareness of something deeper and more close to the bone of existence. At this level, it is closer to intuition than to knowledge, properly so-called. Quite often, the moral meaning has its roots in this sense of the numinous; a sense that there are values in life, frequently unarticulated; a sense that life must be lived in accordance with certain standards, religious or natural. This "knowledge" ties together the individual, society and God, and dictates one's actions in accordance with that order of things.

From knowledge comes confidence, a sense that what one does is right and good. This also is an aspect of "fear of the Lord." Prov 3:5–7 puts it succinctly: one's own knowledge and judgement can be valuable as long as they are in accord with "truth", personal (God) or abstract (what is identifiable with the divine order). Because of this, "fear" is essentially a relationship. It is a personal attitude to God and to his creation, close and intelligent. Fear of Yahweh becomes reliance upon him (Prov 3:5), and acceptance of the fact that there exist values and standards outside of oneself but related to him. Essentially, then, "fear" is a commitment to God, and a knowledge of what one is committed to. This attitude leads to wisdom, enabling one to acquire it. It would be more correct to see the classic statement, "fear of Yahweh, that is wisdom", as a parallel rather than as an equation. They are not to be identified; they serve to define and expand each other. Fear is a steady, ongoing relationship with God. By this fact it stands almost as a summary of the attitude of the wise person, for after all one does not live one's life in the Temple precincts but on the street and in one's home, at everyday tasks. The basic relationship of order must apply equally clearly there, for it is there that character is formed, that one has one's sphere of influence, that one achieves goodness.

Essentially, it teaches us something about faith at its real level, by stressing its relational aspect. Faith is an attitude to something experienced. The number of actions one can justify exclusively on the basis of theological faith is small; thus one must have a *sense of what is right* in a given situation, even if clear rules are unavailable. Experience thus liberates faith. So "fear" is a form of conscience that calls for an intellectual adhesion to a principle, the divine order, the concept of goodness of life, and this is a guarantee of "success." This is strongly influenced by the individualist trend in Wisdom: each one must have a means of living his own life according to personal standards. So it is a knowledge of, and a respect for, elementary moral norms, implying an intellectual capacity to recognize these norms, and motivated by a personal relationship with a known God. Respect for universal moral principles is in its own way respect for God, and "fear" of him. Essentially, it is a vertical relationship that affects one's activity on the horizontal level.

So "fear of Yahweh" is not primarily motivated by a concept of retribution or forensic justice, but by a personal relationship with one who imposes the imperatives of the moral law on the human conscience. Thus it is a standard of moral conduct implying knowledge of one's human status and of its implications. It might well be called a good, formed, sense of what religion and humanity imply in everyday life. It is a sense of what is right or wrong that derives from one's knowledge of a personal involvement with God. As such, it is seen by the sages as honest reflection on the best way to dominate the human environment.

As the term is used in the sapiential tradition certain things stand out: the substantival form is used absolutely—it is a *state of mind,* not an action; it is almost synonymous with *knowledge* (especially in Prov 1—9); and it is often used in parallel to the concept "integrity," or right moral comportment. In the later wisdom writings such as Job (28) and Sirach, and perhaps Ps 112(111), it becomes a complex concept that includes a sense of the mystery of life, a warm, human relationship with God and with the phenomena of experience (true also of the deuteronomistic school), and a consequent moral sense of what is right—the "natural law" inscribed in conscience. Job 27:6 speaks of this internal norm—"my heart does not reproach me for any of my days", and Sir 42:18 reflects the same point of view. Sir 44:1—50:24, the well-known "praise of famous men", speaks of a righteousness and piety based on both *Tôrah* and an internal norm—understanding, wisdom and instruction. Qoheleth reflects a theism all its own, and a "fear of the Lord" (8:10–13), but his real assessment of righteousness is founded on a concept of universal morality and an empiric sense of the "right" (8:1—9:17). This moral sense is an awareness of the fact that human experience is the key to knowledge, and that there is no experience that does not include faith if one is a believer in the divinity. Included is the equally important perception that there is no faith that does not rest on a personal perception, and result in a personal way of acting. The great "apologia" of Job 31 may stand as a classic eulogy of the natural conscience. In a solemn declaration of innocence Job reveals an ideal of ethical consciousness, brought out by the opening words of v. 1a: "I have made a covenant with my eyes", which implies an exceptionally developed level of inner awareness of the "right."

With the concept of "fear of Yahweh" it can be seen that in the wisdom tradition faith is seen to liberate knowledge, by adding a more comprehensive dimension to knowledge—a feeling for the breadth of human experience.

The Personification of Wisdom.

An unusual feature of Old Testament literature is the figure of personified wisdom, found especially in Proverbs, Sirach and Wisdom, but occurring elsewhere in a less marked manner. It appears to be uniquely Israelite since it does not occur in Egyptian parallels, where wisdom remains at most a human attribute, with no abstract value. There are two reasons for the process of personification: as poetic diction, to add emphasis, or vividness to an idea; and as a stylistic device to express certain abstract qualities inherent in the object. Both these aspects may be found in the Bible, for example Ps 85 (84) personifies certain divine attributes. One thing, however, that marks the sapiential use of the device is the recurring factor of "wisdom" preaching in the streets. Prov 1:20 introduces Wisdom in significant terms: "Wisdom cries aloud in the street; in the markets she raises her voice", and with minor modifications the idea is taken up again in 8:1–3 and 9:3. Again, Sir 24:1 speaks of personified Wisdom in similar terms: "Wisdom will praise herself, and will glorify herself in the midst of the people." This concept is possibly due to the fact that it is in idle hours spent "on street corners" that youth is most vulnerable, and therefore of concern to the teacher; but it is also true that the proper place for Wisdom to make her abode is in the arena of everyday living, for it is practical in its aim. It proposes to change the quality of one's life, not the manner.

As an educational device, it is used by the teachers of Israel very effectively. The young are encouraged to approach the task of education with a degree of personal commitment—to make wisdom one's bride, to go to her house and attain a degree of intimacy with learning. In this way the goal of education is seen to be the distillation of a quality of life. Indeed, many of the characteristics of the figure of "Lady Wisdom" have been adapted from the attributes of the teacher or parent, and even of the lesson being taught.

However, the texts of Proverbs, Job, Sirach, Baruch and Wisdom have another reason. They see the search for knowledge and control—the process of learning—from a new, and more intellectualized angle. Wisdom has a unique relationship with the created world, so one finds life by finding wisdom, and thus ultimately one finds God.

The personification of wisdom is thus meant to expand and clarify the teaching of the sages by identifying that teaching with something more exalted, the source of wisdom. This is seen in the shared vocabulary of the instruction and the personification texts. Wisdom reflects one particular quality of the divinity, it is to some degree unattainable. Job 28 is quite explicit, as in vv 12–14:

> But where shall wisdom be found? And where is the place of understanding?
> Man does not know the way to it, and it is not found in the land of the living.
> The deep says, "It is not in me", and the sea says, "It is not with me."

Bar 3:29–31 expresses the same belief:

> Who has gone up into heaven, and taken her,
> and brought her down from the clouds?
> Who has gone over the sea, and found her,
> and will buy her for pure gold?
> No one knows the way to her,
> or is concerned about the path to her;

and Sir 1:1 claims that "All wisdom comes from the Lord", and 1:6 asks, "The root of wisdom—to whom has it been revealed? Her clever devices—who knows them?" One can achieve so much; even if much remains unattainable one can achieve some grasp of things (Job 28), but it remains impossible to come to the source of "wisdom" itself—unless that "source" takes the initiative and comes to man. Thus the wisdom project attains its goal. The human being is provoked by his world; he sets out to grasp and master it, intellectually first, then practically; in this process he discovers that by its own nature it is reaching out to him, for it was created in relation to him; so surrender to wisdom is integration with the totality of being. This to the Hebrew is never a totally conceptual process, for the language was incapable of functioning in this way; essentially, it had to be a personal process, at the level of "knowing", the existential act.

One might ask, who or what is personified wisdom? The image is far too flexible and rich to be tied down to any one meaning. It can represent wisdom teaching itself (Prov 1:20), or the universalized value of instruction (Prov 8:1, see below, p. 146), or the primeval or cosmic order (also Prov 8). It is sister (Prov 7:4), guide (Prov 6:22) and gracious hostess (Prov 9:1–6); it can represent a divine "emanation" or "hypostasis" (as in Prov 9), or the Law given to Israel (Bar 3:9–14 and Sir 24:1–19). Some authors see her as representing Israel herself. In fact, "Lady Wisdom" is not totally identifiable with any single idea. It is used by different authors to meet the needs of different circumstances, and its flexibility makes it ideally suited to this task.

Central to a proper understanding of the phenomenon of personification is the fact of an abstract name being used. Yahweh is himself wise, and he desires a relationship to man, so his wisdom becomes a dynamic of relationship, and so a person. The personification emphasizes the desirability of wisdom, something that is so personal it must be acquired if one seeks life. Wisdom thus becomes a force in which God makes himself present and in which he wishes to be sought. Indeed, Prov 8:35 shows Wisdom speaking as if she were God, yet she is a creature and remains separate from him. In this way she serves the sages as a bond between the created universe and God, and maintains a line of relationship with the universe and with its creator. In Prov 8, in fact, the world presents itself to humanity as a moral order that is personified, and represents the communicative aspect of world order. Though it is not God who speaks here, Prov 8 is stylistically a divine statement of self-revelation. Wisdom is a channel by which God can reach out to humanity, and draw humanity to himself, led by the voice of creation and the inherent mystery of creation. This is a very sapiential perception.

Thus the personification of wisdom represents a particular aspect of the divinity—the desire to integrate human secular life and the divine. Being a witness of, and participator in creation (Prov 8:22–31), Wisdom can act as mediator for all. It becomes a way of internationalizing the vocation to wisdom, for there is something primordial about her that attracts all. Prov 9 shows how the human mind sets out on its programme of understanding its world, meets the divine "influence" behind the order of the world and does so *on a personal level.* This concept of a courtship of Wisdom by mankind is a recurrent theme in sapiential literature: Sir 14; 15; 51; Wis 6; 8. In Prov 8 another aspect of Lady Wisdom is shown—a relationship of *love* that she has with humanity. It represents the surrender of men to the love of "existence" and the mystery of creation that is an image of the divinity. According to Sir 24:7–11 Wisdom has "pitched her tent in Israel" and resides among the people (see also Bar 3:37). The reason given is that they, and only they, were willing and equipped to "listen" to her.

In the Old Testament the personification of wisdom took on a special function. Through her the created, material world has a voice, and can articulate "the glory of God", Ps 19 (18), not in prayer as such, but simply by being a creature. The world, in all its ramifications, gives a real witness to the divine because behind it and in it wisdom "rejoices like a child" (Prov 8). But it does not, even here, address this praise *to God*; rather, Lady Wisdom addresses herself *to mankind,* and shows what she is capable of, and what the reader is capable of if only he accepts the invitation of v. 32—"and now . . . listen to me"; for through her the individual can "find life" (v. 35), and become whole.

This is the point of the feminine personification. It raises the wisdom quest to a mystical level, and makes of it a vehicle of spirituality through which God commits his presence to man (Prov 4:4–8). The reality he is offered corresponds to his intellectual need (which in a way initiated the search). The "female" element of spirituality is here predominant. It introduces a dialectic of mutuality (Sir 51), leading to a quasi-mystical immersion of the learner into the divinity. In fact, this chapter of Sirach associates the sage's love of learning with his desire for God in semi-mystical terms, as a surrender to a presence that possessed him (see also Canticle of Canticles with regard to the way words are used). Sirach clearly expands Proverb's concept of the search for wisdom to the point where it takes on all the characteristics of a search for a lover. The author sees the most humanly attractive element in the divinity to be analogous to the feminine in humanity. Thus knowledge of wisdom becomes more than an intellectual perception—it is a personal gift of one human being to another "being". The connection with the transcendent, so achieved, is seen by the later editors of Proverbs as a courtship, and a winning of the feminine manifestation of the divinity. Wisdom herself takes the same theological line: she is an "emanation of the Most High"; she makes herself perceptible to those who court her (who make the effort to attain to wisdom); and she leads them to participate in her own eternal scope with God. Wisdom, here, is a "daughter" of God, and so a lover of men, leading to personal possession on a humanly perceptible level.

The Secular.

Historically, Israel's awareness of God's creational role was a relatively late development. The concept of God as Creator can of course be found in earlier strata of the Old Testament. For example, both Gen 2:4b–25 (the Yahwistic tradition from the tenth century B.C.) and Isa 17:7 (from the eighth century) recognize God as "Maker", creator of the world and of mankind. But this may be taken as a residue of non-Israelite mythology, and it had little real influence on theology until it was taken up later by the Priestly tradition and Deutero-Isaiah, with their concept of the creative "word" of Yahweh—an idea not found so explicitly in earlier traditions. Proverbs speaks of God as "maker" (14:31; 17:5; 22:2), as does Job, a wisdom book with a different perspective (4:17; 32:22; 35:10). This perception of creation resulted in a new way of looking at God and man, distinct from the redemption theology of the older traditions (compare Jer 2:6–7 and 27:5–6). It expressed a distinctive religious idea—the primacy of the human being in the world of the human. Wisdom was more than commonly aware of this fact, that God had created mankind free and responsible: Gen 1 explicitly gives mankind *dominion* over the created world (vv. 28–30), an idea lacking to the Yahwistic tradition of Gen 2. This perception led to an emphasis on the secular, which was seen by the sages as involving a call to maturity, a call to live *in* the world rather than *over against* it. Life was presented, to a great degree, as a human enterprise.

The first fruit of this perception was a particular way of looking at society and at government. This can be seen in Proverbs and in Sirach. Prov 16:10–15 and 22:1–4 present a social scene dominated by human values and human life (see below, p. 181), while Sir 10 presents the wise ruler in human terms, while acknowledging his share in the divine dominion. Actually, it may be that changed circumstances made such a secular outlook necessary. For example, Saul and the earlier kings of Israel (the monarchy began with Saul towards the end of the eleventh century) could have recourse to ritual oracles and symbols such as the Urim and Thummim (see 1 Sam 14:41; also Exod 28:30), but in a more pluralist world (such as that of the Jew of the Exile) this was no longer viable. In the world conceived by the sages a ruler, a teacher, a government official had to be able to act as did the scribes of an earlier age in Egypt; he could not wait for a new revelation or a new divine intervention. So grew an awareness that God tended to leave much of day-to-day affairs to responsible agents. But this was not necessarily a smooth transition, for people tend to feel uncomfortable when the old, firmly declared norms in religion give way to a new form of "liberalism"; quite often they simply do not know how to cope. This might very well be the situation that lies behind the final redaction of Proverbs, for example.

However, a more lasting result of all this changed perspective was a new insight: the individual's theological independance. Wisdom saw the human being as one who is emancipated; one who would have to make his own decisions and was free to do so—and of course, this was one who would have to live with the consequences. The literature that found something of its inspiration in this idea clearly recognized human power, and also human limitations (Prov 16:1, 9). But over and above all there grew up a trust in man's capacity to cope—and of his own ability, not just by occasional grace (Qoh 11).

Thus wisdom became concerned with the individual and his scope, rather than with the theologically dominated concept of "people of God". This resulted in a morality dominated by the created nature of the human being, and not by the transcendent nature of the Creator. In fact, an "existential morality" of the human being and the world, as Sirach suggests in 17:2–8; after all, God gave human beings "tongue and eyes; he gave them ears and a mind for thinking. He filled them with knowledge and understanding, and showed them good and evil" (vv. 6–7. See also Wis 9:2; 10:2). It was seen to be the human vocation to go out and master the world (Gen 1), and while *Tôrah* expressed this in creation narratives, Wisdom took it up by asking the very practical question—how? The answer was—by counsel, Prov 11:14; 15:22 and especially 20:18: "Plans are established by counsel; by wise guidance wage war". The *Tôrah* commands, the wise counsel—indeed, *yôʿes* counsellor, was traditionally the designation of the sage. And his weightiest argument was human reason and practical experience. What is good?, what is expedient?, above all, *what is seen to work?* Thus while law commands one to go out and establish the things of God, wisdom instructs one to establish the things of the world. This may be effectively done by approaching the perceptible data of experience, controlling them by knowledge, and adapting oneself to them by judgement (Prov 20:1–11). So the wisdom teacher set out to make observations on the particular kinds of action that could affect human situations, and so establish the viability, and the value, of human life—achieve "goodness". Rooted in experience, one grows to realize that certain things "just do not work".

So wisdom becomes a human art of life, in the sense that it did not set up a dream world, a world of the "purely ideal", but tried to master life *as it was experienced,* within the very real framework of a specific order, and without specific reference to the divine sphere. The starting point tended to be anthropological. And for this reason it is in the wisdom tradition that the question of theodicy rises most emphatically; much of the rest of the biblical tradition could answer it on the basis of "faith", but Wisdom had to argue it more from reason and experience. The answer, in so far as one is possible, lies in the perception that retribution is to some degree founded on the fact that the world has been committed to man, and that history and its shaping is up to him—he will therefore reap precisely what he sows. One book in particular emerges from an explicit theology of creation, Qoheleth. The author starts off with the *fact* of creation—the world as a received phenomenon—rather than with the divine initiative, though of course there is the recognition that "he created it beautiful in its time" (3:11). He accepts the wisdom principle that man is in the world to dominate it, but he sees that this dominion is always limited. The only logical reaction is some form of surrender to being.

The faith of the Old Testament is centered on a historical act of encounter, God's gift of self-revelation which is continued in history. This is the first thing that marks out the wisdom tradition as distinctive, for it is essentially free of this historical, revelatory dimension. However, it would be wrong to think of Wisdom as a purely secular discipline; it exists always in an ambient of faith. This is seldom explicit, and is not emphasized, but it does exert a certain influence. Mankind has still a religious commitment—but the parameters have changed.

The Book of Proverbs

INTRODUCTION

The Book of Proverbs is a mirror held up to life. It is timeless, in the sense that it is not addressed to any one age or people, but to all ages and every sort of person. In fact, one of the attractions of Proverbs is that it appeals to what is most basic in everyday life. Open-minded, it has something of value to say about the world we all live in, irrespective of religious or political affiliation, in that it teaches us how to live well on this earth: as a citizen, a parent, a worker; how to be a teacher, or an artist; and how to live with your God.

The religion of Proverbs is not obtrusive; the sectarian has little place. It approaches holiness as a matter of fact, calling, not for a change of lifestyle or a conversion, but for a deeper quality in *any* way of life. Much of its teaching applies equally to the pagan as to the believer.

> Trust in the Lord with all your heart,
> and do not rely on your own insight.
> In all your ways acknowledge him,
> and he will make straight your paths.
> Be not wise in your own eyes;
> fear the Lord, and turn away from evil.
>
> (Prov 3:5–7)

Change "Lord" to "lord", and this is a statement of universal validity. In effect, it is a religious humanism, and even the most particularized teaching is part of a whole regime the aim of which is simply the formation of a human being.

What is a Proverb?

The "proverb" is a literary form found throughout the Bible, frequently outside of the book called Proverbs (e.g. Num 21:27–30; 23:7; Isa 14:4; Ezek 17:2). All of these differ in scope, and this is the first indication of the real richness this art-form achieved in the Old Testament. Diverse as they are, all have two things in common: a basic similarity, and a moral implication.

Technically, a proverb—*mashal* in Hebrew—is a likeness, perceived or imposed, between two or more phenomena. For example, Prov 15:4, "a gentle tongue is like a tree of life". Morally, the comparison serves to bring out the *inner* meaning or value of something or some action. Thus a proverb, from the biblical point of view, is usually a moral or religious teaching, based on experience or observation, common or personal, and communicated by means of similarity. The structure is normally binary—a unit (normally a verse) compounded of two parts—and parallel. Prov 10:10 is a good example:

> He who winks the eye causes trouble,
> but he who boldly reproves makes peace.

This is a "true proverb", as distinct from the "instruction" type frequently found, which is generally a longer unit, almost a short essay, such as may be found in 1:10–19. The proverb presents an inner tension of contrast. From this dialectic of perceived and implied a new perception arises. Normally, since a proverb supplies no more than the thesis (the phenomenon as perceived) and the antithesis (the implication) of any dialectic, the reader or listener must think for himself so as to arrive at a synthesis and so learn something. Prov 20:4 is an example:

> The sluggard does not plow in the autumn;
> he will seek at harvest and have nothing.

Here the thesis is something observed, the fact that if one does not plow one can expect no reward; the actual situation is agrarian. There follows the implication that there lies in this a principle that is applicable to all walks of life. It remains for the reader or listener to arrive at a synthesis: how can this principle apply in my particular situation?

Even this synthesis will not be normative, and need not be the same for everyone who hears or reads the proverb. Each individual's life-situation differs to some extent, and each person has something personal to bring to a proverb. Any given proverb may teach something slightly different to different readers, since the quality of each person's experience, and perception of similarity, differs. Prov 14:20 is a somewhat cynical judgement, but it depends on an individual experience and the extent to which each one carries the similarity:

> The poor is disliked even by his neighbour,
> but the rich has many friends.

Basically, then, a proverb comes to us as a likeness between phenomena. By extension it can be a play on ideas, as 20:2: "The dread wrath of a king is like the growling of a lion; he who provokes him to anger forfeits his life"; or even an implicit comparison, as 21:11: "When a scoffer is punished, the simple becomes wise". Thus the term "proverb" in its Old Testament context can take on an extended meaning. It is applied to short, pithy sayings that merely preserve the binary rhythm and parallelism of the true proverb, and even to sapiential sayings or sentences that are at an even further remove from the strict meaning of the term, to enigmatic sayings and epigrams and caricatures.

The intellectual dimension of this type of didactic literature is important. Traditionally, it presents a sage, parent or teacher who, out of his or her knowledge of the mysteries of life, speaks to a pupil in the name of cosmic or social order and good sense. It is seldom directly imperative, since the hearer bases his actions on his own judgement, his own assessment of the situation and the applicability of the proverb. The sanctions, where they occur, are seldom external; the human act has its own repercussions. The central concept is basic—human existence is part of a fundamentally stable order, and all one need do is act sensibly. In many proverbs definite judgements are expressed, normally by means of the binary formula "better is . . . than", for example 17:1. In some others the teacher states a specific instance of experience and the reader thinks it out. In this way one can gain a knowledge of the world and of humanity, and even if one cannot explain why certain eventualities occur, knowing about them serves to make one aware of the complexity of life.

Some of the proverbs are clearly *didactic* in tone, as for the most part chapters 12 and 13. Equally clearly, others have a primarily *literary* function, being the distillation of human experience, and its subsequent articulation as an art form.

> To get wisdom is better than gold;
> to get understanding is to be chosen rather
> than silver
>
> (16:16)

These latter can also be didactic, but one gets the decided impression that pleasure in words/images is the author's first intention. Strictly speaking the *mashal* must be an artform: had it not been crafted with some care, and adequately, it would not have been preserved. Sometimes, indeed, the emphasis seems to be more on style than on substance; 26:14–15 must have given a deal of sly pleasure to author as well as audience. Proverbs tend to have this other side to them, they are in their way an entertainment. Structurally, the artistic form predominates. Beyond that, many are witty, malicious or even simply playful. Verse 27:15 is *meant* to be humorous, and to take proverbs such as this soberly is to lose their value. They are amusing insights into our common human nature:

> "It is bad, it is bad", says the buyer;
> but when he goes away, then he boasts.(20:14)

a picture of each one of us who has picked up a bargain. The ultimate form where this is found is the riddle, popular in proverbial literature.

To recall the overall place of Proverbs in sapiential literature, it is suggestive that while "proverb" in Hebrew primarily means a "comparison", it is from the root *mshl,* which means "to dominate" something. Art form they certainly are, but one must never lose sight of the function of wisdom—the domination of the human environment. The proverb served this end. It became a sapiential form that supplied standards of behaviour based on an appreciation of the order and design in creation.

How to Approach a Proverb

An examination of the literary pre-history of the genre shows the basic construction of a proverb: first an observation of phenomena, a perception of likeness, co-ordination of the data, and finally a statement of truth; 15:19. This determines how the reader must approach it: first a labour of synthesis, then a perception of universality. It is this latter that makes it a proverb.

There are two ways in which the reader's own personal experience can expand the meaning of a proverb. Prov 14:13 is one of the most beautiful in the collection:

> Even in laughter the heart is sad,
> and the end of joy is grief.

What is the reader's perception of joy or sorrow? It depends on one's own experience of the sorrows of life. So the proverb-form *can deepen the emotional intensity of an idea* by relating it to experience, and can retrospectively deepen the emotional intensity *of the experience itself* by opening it up to meaning. Again, a different kind of proverb reflects a particular situation; 10:5:

> A son who gathers in summer is prudent,
> but a son who sleeps in harvest brings shame;

yet this particular "situation proverb" can allow one to perceive the central truth in a *general human situation,* or other analogous situations.

From the very form of the proverb it can be seen that its function is not directly to teach, but to make one think effectively about life. That its primary aim is to provoke thought is evident from the fact that many are put in contradictory terms, for example 26:4–5.

> Answer not a fool according to his folly,
> lest you be like him yourself.
> Answer a fool according to his folly,
> lest he be wise in his own eyes.

The reader must ask: which applies in *my* situation? One is not meant to be passive, a mere receptacle for the teacher's wisdom, but an active collaborator in learning from experience. Rather than inculcating a spirit of docility, the proverb is often an invitation to contestation, pupil versus teacher. Whose mind is faster? They are meant to be a process of learning, never an abdication of one's own intelligence and judgement. Thus reading Proverbs is an existential experience. One does not learn *from* them but *by means of* them, for through the suggestive power of language one reaches the reality they seek to express. Addressed to the individual, their teaching is applicable to anyone in an analogous situation.

The implication of many proverbs is the existence of a relationship of similarity between two (or more) phenomena lying on different planes, which raises one's perception of the human environment. Take the real depth of a proverb such as 27:17. Here is an undoubted perception of both nature and the human being. By speaking in pictures, however, it enables the reader to lay hold of an *evident* phenomenon, and make a mental link with something similar on a deeper level. Thus one pushes forward to a deeper comprehension beyond the words.

Date and Composition.

In judging the date and the originality of the *Book of Proverbs* we must remember two things: the actual material itself, and the editorial project.

The actual material, both proverb-type and instruction-type, could in fact belong to any age. However, comparison with similar literature from Egypt and Mesopotamia, and linguistic comparison with Ugaritic (a language related to Hebrew and spoken in Phoenicia and Canaan), suggests that most of the material is quite early, pre-exilic, and some of it even pre-monarchic.

Most authorities recognize five collections in the book, but close dating is extremely difficult. The first two collections are said to be "proverbs of Solomon", 1:1 and again in 10:1. This attribution is a literary device, and very little help in dating. In fact, the first collection, 1:1—9:18, is on the whole the work of later editors, and may date from the 5th to the 4th centuries B.C. It is the final editor's introduction to the whole work. The second collection, 10:1—22:16, exhibits a simplicity of form that suggests an early, pre-exilic date, although it is possible that minor variations and additions were made by the final editor. The "Sayings of the Wise", 22:17—24:22 may be from the same period as the first nine chapters. There is a return to the intimate, parental style, and the Egyptian influence is noticeable. Most authorities accept some form of dependance on the Egyptian *Instruction of Amen-em-ope*. Like this latter text, Prov 22:17—24:22 may be sub-divided into "thirty sayings of admonition and knowledge" (Prov 22:20), and the style, that of parental advice, is much similar. Many of the sayings themselves duplicate sayings in *Amen-em-ope*. The Egyptian text is a sophisticated manual of instruction for aspiring scribes and scholars, and probably dates from the 11th to the 10th centuries B.C. The short collection entitled "These also are sayings of the wise" (24:23–34) seems to be an appendix to the previous collection, and by the same author. There is little reason to question the attribution of the final collection (25:1—29:27), "These also are proverbs of Solomon which the men of Hezekiah king of Judah copied" (25:1). This places the final section of the book in the 8th century B.C. The four appendices in 30:1—31:31 contain some older material, but show signs of having been given their final form by the editors of the book.

Thus, while much of the material, and indeed some of the collections, are old, the actual Book of Proverbs as we have it was put together, and in part modified, at a quite late period, and reflects a post-exilic editorial intention to some degree. The final "edition" shows the usual influence of academic universalism. More perhaps than any other book in the Old Testament, Proverbs provides an overview of wisdom from the oral stage to the most sophisticated international and "intellectual" stage of Later Wisdom.

This long period of gestation, as it were, is in part responsible for the occasional weaknesses of the book. To some extent it represents a world that no longer exists, and some of its values no longer apply, just as some few of its perspectives are limited by its origins. However, rooted in the most basic of human values as it is, it remains a formidably rich and profound document.

For the same reason there is a certain lack of consistency throughout in the use of technical terms, such as "simple", "fool" and even "wise". The term "simple"—in Hebrew *peta'îm*—is frequently used in Proverbs. Primarily it refers to a young person; someone who is untrained, lacking education, even ingenuous. Such a one is thought to be susceptible to the sage's instruction, as also to perverse influence (1:4). The fool is something else (1:7). He is the opposite to the wise person, totally indocile to man and to God. He may lack intelligence, but this is not necessarily so. What marks him in the sapiential tradition is a rejection of learning and instruction, and consequently sometimes a rejection of Yahweh. He is malicious and uncontrolled of tongue (10:14), perverse in human relationship (20:3) and of unbridled temper (12:16). He remains closed, and incorrigible. Somewhere between these comes the "scoffer" (9:7–8). Volatility is his main characteristic. He is too flippant, and sometimes too arrogant, or insolent, to listen and therefore indisposed to learn (13:1). Too superficial to achieve wisdom, he remains an adolescent all his life (14:6). While all of these types retain a basic meaning in the wisdom of the Old Testament, they are, especially in Proverbs, somewhat adaptable. They may be applied with varying nuances of meaning in different situations. The same is true even of the most basic term "wise". While this has a fundamental meaning, the emphasis may change from situation to situation. Often the context will determine whether moral or intellectual maturity is in question, or practical sagacity or knowledge. A document that originates in different ages and at different hands may be expected to show a certain variety of implication.

By the time Proverbs assumed its final form the wisdom writers had succeeded in bridging the gap between their discipline and that of the priests and lawyers, and had therefore succeeded in uniting the two systems of education—civil and religious. They could thus write 1:1–7 as a "preface" to the work, combining the secular tradition (vv. 2–6) with the religious (v. 7). The two types of learning became united, and these first seven verses present the credentials of the "wise". The first nine chapters present the most sophisticated concept of wisdom in the whole book, and are more deliberately theological, possibly due to the fact that the editors saw the need for an accommodation with the more religious traditions of Israel. The collections in 10—22 and 25—29 are more secular, indeed almost totally secular, since religion takes a subordinate place. We seem to have a deliberate effort at integrating secular wisdom and religious conviction. The name of Yahweh, for example, is frequently inserted into older material at key points to modify the thrust.

The Intention of the Editors.

Proverbs, in spite of its rag-tag appearance, is in fact dominated by the common intention of its editors: to lead people by ways of uprightness, intelligence and religious "backbone" to fulness of life.

The problems of the book are those that face all of us living in a world of daily concerns: a decent level of subsistence; other human beings with their foibles and frailties; a God who often remains incomprehensible. How can one achieve a more fulfilled life?, attain one's potentialities?, live with the mystery? So the raw materials for Proverbs is the human person living in contact with the realities of nature and the limitations they impose; the necessary compromise forced on us by human nature. On the whole, we are given an optimistic view on mankind, and a conviction that human intelligence and reason *can* achieve something worthwhile.

The final redaction presents a world-view that is marked by the sages' open-minded respect for knowledge and intelligence; for speculative curiosity as well as for practical success. The fascination that all of visible nature had for them bears testimony to this spirit. Because of this, the first book in the sapiential literature recovers a "lost" spirituality: fear of God, confidence in humanity, respect for creation, allied to an intellectual commitment to all that wisdom implies. The desire for learning becomes a positive religious attitude: "the fear of the Lord is the beginning of wisdom, and the knowledge of the Holy One is insight".

Book I
The Proverbs of Solomon Son of David
1:1—9:18

THE FIRST COLLECTION OF PROVERBS 1:1—9:18

This first collection, entitled "The Proverbs of Solomon, son of David, king of Israel", has a deliberate didactic purpose. It reaches out to all those who have even the slightest disposition to learn the meaning of life and the way of human success. Addressed to a people who have need of a viable philosophy of life, it reflects the teaching preoccupation: how to inculcate a sense of values, how to provide stability to a generation that has grown estranged from its religious roots and social structures. It is thus an effort at winning both the good will and the obedience of a people by presenting the best their cultural and religious traditions have to offer—wisdom itself. And it presents wisdom under two guises: the instruction of a teacher/parent personally involved with the reader; and a personified wisdom who appeals directly, and even emotionally, to mankind. The moral teaching is practical and indeed simple: avoidance of bad company; knowledge of one's duty to God and to society; prudence and self-control; and above all, love of learning and truth. This is relatively class-less, addressed to anyone willing to listen and learn, and it shows the true value of humanism. To this are added sections that refer to God, less as the divinity *in se* than as a motive for proper behaviour and a source of wisdom, as well as maxims and proverbs of a practical nature.

CHAPTER 1

THE INTELLECTUAL ADVENTURE. 1:1–7.

These verses of introduction present a doctrinal resumé of the whole collection, almost all of the elements of the book being found here, along with the basic principle that the one who finds wisdom finds life. In the mind of the final editor the rest of Proverbs must be, indeed can only be, understood in terms of the guidelines found here. So we are given a broad plan of action and study whose purpose is to enable mankind to establish a proper relationship with God from its own particular situation in life, and old (secular) wisdom is carefully blended with a more formal religious sense so as to achieve this end.

The Title. 1:1.

1 The proverbs of Solomon, son of David,
king of Israel.

The superscription "Proverbs of Solomon" is not meant to indicate authorship but to remind the reader of the richness of the wisdom heritage now placed before him. Even the use of the word "proverb" somewhat obscures the nature of the work which contains several literary types, including instructions and sentences. However, it does remind the pupil of the first requisite: personal application. What follows is geared to any person willing to be educated, and is a unity, as may be seen from the grammatical structure—the infinite construct that dominates the rest of the passage linking vv. 2–6 to v. 1.

The Prologue. 1:2–6.

[2]That men may know wisdom and
instruction,
understand words of insight,
[3]receive instruction in wise dealing,
righteousness, justice, and equity;
[4]that prudence may be given to the
simple,
knowledge and discretion to the
youth—
[5]the wise man also may hear and
increase in learning,
and the man of understanding
acquire skill,
[6]to understand a proverb and a figure,
the words of the wise and their
riddles.

We are introduced to wisdom, and find it a complex, and fascinating concept. It could very well be translated "excellence", that quality compounded of skill, knowledge, judgement and a mystic insight that raises a person above the common rank. It aims at creating leaders in society and world builders. The sages here have a very wide scope. They invite the reader to possess wisdom, interiorize it and communicate it, and they set out to do this by provoking the curiosity of the pupil. "Wisdom" (v. 2) is both innate and acquired, and may be gained by learning, by keeping the company of the wise, and above all by discipline. Through education one *can* make something of oneself.

The editors have clearly determined their audience, and

indeed the general audience of the book—those willing to learn, even if they *are* the "simple" (v. 4); those who can be led and are docile; those who know that they have something to learn. With this basic attitude one can master life and take one's place in the world.

And the sages begin well: prescinding from the religious considerations they are concerned with mastery, and this begins with *mastery of oneself*. In v. 2 we find the vocabulary of Old Wisdom, indicative of a tough educational discipline productive of rigorous intellectual values. The term *musar,* "discipline", implies receptivity and a willingness to work. It deals with empirically based wisdom, drawn from the teacher's greater experience, and hence his authority. This is the first note of realism. Wisdom does not come easily, one must be willing to make sacrifices for it, integrate mind and heart. Here the chain of authority is natural, not imposed. Given human nature, one needs a master, and an obedience to him. The process of formation is clear: the growth of a human person from pupil to learner to adept, culminating in a "wise" person capable of making a way through life.

No one term is adequate to describe the finished product, so a veritable "symphony" of related concepts (vv. 2b-5) is given that expands and develops the idea "wisdom". "Insight" and "wise dealing", a kind of balanced judgement, a *savoir-faire* that is in fact the external manifestation of understanding. "Discretion" also is needed, for being thought "practical" can have pejorative overtones. But worldly wisdom is not necessarily a bad thing, for the secular has its value. The interest here is in building intellectual and moral maturity so that a pupil can take a stable place in the world that he has to live in. Actually, vv. 4 and 5 go together, and form a composite picture of a person who has "acquired skill". The emphasis is on v. 5, where the Hebrew word *tahbulôt,* translated "skill", signifies one "who knows the ropes" like a good helmsman.

The first step is openness to learning, but it does not stop there. According to the sages the reader had to steep himself in the accumulated wisdom of the ages, in his own traditions and in a respect for alien traditions, so that personal judgements might be made on a solid basis. *First* achieve expertise, and *then* when you go through life you may do things your own way and be effective. In v. 6 the form as well as the content is important, for we have here the sort of language in which traditionally wisdom and knowledge were passed on, and it says the last word with simple dignity: if you *do* it or *say* it, do so as well as can be done, with flair!

The Motive. 1:7.

> [7]The fear of the LORD is the
> beginning of knowledge;
> fools despise wisdom and
> instruction.

The previous section dealt for the most part with the intellectual qualities of perception, judgement and control. This context is now transformed by v. 7, which closes the prefatory section by giving a purely religious impetus to the pupil's endeavour—the "new *musar*" or discipline of "fear of the Lord". This serves as a connecting link between the Prologue and the subsequent discourses in 1:8—9:18. Found again in a modified form in 9:10, it supplies an essential key to the mind of the editors. "Beginning" in the context means first principle, so knowledge worth the reader's effort begins with a religious motivation. Since the proper name "Yahweh" is used it is probably a question of a personal aspect of religion. This idea counteracts what might have been seen as a too secular motive for the pursuit of wisdom in vv. 2–6.

This has already been hinted at in v. 3, which, like v. 7, belongs to Later Wisdom. In both cases we find a much more theological vocabulary. The two terms "righteousness" (*sedeq*) and "justice" (*mishpat*) in v. 3 belong to the language of piety. However, together they form the object of the verb "receive", so they can be learned. Already this verse, the only one in the section that modifies secular wisdom by introducing a religious note, sets a prefatory tone. The context is the search for wisdom, predominantly secular and intellectual, and now this is further qualified by "fear" of God—a religious attitude, and because of the word "insight", an effective one. With this idea we come closest to the editorial policy of the authors of Prov 1—9. Now it is a religious attitude that leads to "life" (an idea shared by Ps 34 [33]).

So the motive that drives the reader on this quest for "wisdom" is not as simple as might appear. The end result is still success in the human sphere, but the term must be reinterpreted. In Proverbs we have the main wisdom preoccupation—attaining worldly fulfillment, but this is now seen as both external and internal: material, moral, religious are combined, based on the Hebrew concept of the human person as a unity. So here the "wise" and the "righteous" are coterminous. Religion may not be often referred to explicitly in the book, but it permeates the whole. No matter how worldly life is, God is there. Secular ability and knowledge become religious "science", and what is in question is the formation of a secular *and* religious life-style. This gives a new theological perspective to a basically humanist programme. To the richness of a truly worldly existence the sages have added the flavour of a relationship with God. And so one who fails to perceive the value of a rich, full life is indeed a fool.

THE FIRST PARENTAL ADMONITION. 1:8–19.

[8]Hear, my son, your father's
instruction,
and reject not your mother's
teaching;
[9]for they are a fair garland for your
head,

and pendants for your neck.
[10] My son, if sinners entice you,
do not consent.
[11] If they say, "Come with us, let us
lie in wait for blood,
let us wantonly ambush the
innocent;
[12] like Sheol let us swallow them alive
and whole, like those who go
down to the Pit;
[13] we shall find all precious goods,
we shall fill our houses with
spoil;
[14] throw in your lot among us,
we will all have one purse"—
[15] my son, do not walk in the way with
them,
hold back your foot from their
paths;
[16] for their feet run to evil,
and they make haste to shed blood.
[17] For in vain is a net spread
in the sight of any bird;
[18] but these men lie in wait for their
own blood,
they set an ambush for their own
lives.
[19] Such are the ways of all who get
gain by violence;
it takes away the life of its
possessors.

Hard on the heels of the editorial introduction comes a parental exhortation, the first of many that expand the teaching of the opening verses. It sets before the reader a practical choice—good life or bad, the use of one's talents or the waste of them. Life is a gift it would be criminal to misuse. Here we can find the basic tools for living that dominate the rest of the exhortations scattered through the book, and so find a way through the maze of disparate sayings, riddles and sentences that follow—all of which reflect life in miniature. It is formally an "instruction", an imperative (v. 8) followed by a series of motive clauses. The authority wielded by the sage is the most fundamental for all contemporary cultures, that of the parent. The home is the primary educational force in society. It is there that a youth acquires the basic civilized attitudes. The reference to both parents underlines a basic attitude of Proverbs: mother and father are equally responsible for education, and their authority is primary. It is within the family circle that the child establishes the character values on which future success is founded.

The teacher, then, or the sage derives his authority from this, and stands in *loco parentum*. The teaching that follows is a very practical and human wisdom whose value lies in the fact that it inculcates a balanced and intelligent way of life—the keynote of 1—9. The parent/child, teacher/pupil formula of wisdom instruction found in v. 8 is a formal device, of course. "Hear, my son" is more than a rhetorical formula, it expresses the basic exigence for all interpersonal relationships. Probably modelled on the Egyptian instruction, "hearing" is more than a simple act of listening to someone or paying attention to a statement. It is an attitude of openness to what life can teach, and this is emphasized by v. 9. Already in the first didactic verse the tone is set—establish an attitude of docility and flexibility. The sage then presents a picture of a rebel against society. This is not meant to depict a criminal, but rather the mindless adolescent who consorts with the drop-outs on street corners, and jeers at those who have values and wish to live by them (vv. 11–12). Such a one is too self-confident to listen to those who are not "in fashion". Thus it is not strictly an a-religious attitude but an attitude of mindless contempt for human values. And that is why they harm *themselves* (v. 18). Imagining themselves to be worldly-wise, they are in fact dupes. "Life" in v. 19 is taken in the sense of totality of personality.

Parents are the first models of human values, and theirs

is a high authority. They begin the process, the teacher then takes over until the pupil can form his own judgements. So the sage presents a sample case for the reader, allowing him to make his own application. Verse 17 provides a key to this. It is a riddle, sapiential in character: one does not walk into a trap one knows is there, nor does one ruin one's life by failing to learn the right approach to it, and its real meaning. So the first rule is not to leave oneself open to the wrong kind of influence. There is also a moral here: wealth gained by crime, or too easily is not a gauge of human quality. One may be rich, but lacking true wisdom one's life lacks any real value. So, when tempted, be faithful to your moral upbringing. This challenge is personalized by a realistic picture. The sanctions here are clearly natural, rather than religious. Human action is itself pregnant with its own consequences. What is inculcated here is not piety, but a scale of values and a sense of proportion.

LADY WISDOM'S PERSONAL INVITATION. 1:20–33.

[20]Wisdom cries aloud in the street;
in the markets she raises her voice;
[21]on the top of the walls she cries out;
at the entrance of the city gates
she speaks:
[22]"How long, O simple ones, will you
love being simple?
How long will scoffers delight in their
scoffing
and fools hate knowledge?
[23]Give heed to my reproof;
behold, I will pour out my thoughts
to you;
I will make my words known to you.
[24]Because I have called and you refused
to listen,

have stretched out my hand and no
one has heeded,
[25]and you have ignored all my counsel
and would have none of my reproof,
[26]I also will laugh at your calamity;
I will mock when panic strikes you,
[27]when panic strikes you like a storm,
and your calamity comes like a
whirlwind,
when distress and anguish come
upon you.
[28]Then they will call upon me, but I will
not answer;
they will seek me diligently but will
not find me.
[29]Because they hated knowledge
and did not choose the fear of the
LORD,
[30]would have none of my counsel,
and despised all my reproof,
[31]therefore they shall eat the fruit of
their way
and be sated with their own devices.
[32]For the simple are killed by their
turning away,
and the complacence of fools
destroys them;
[33]but he who listens to me will dwell
secure
and will be at ease, without dread
of evil.''

It is fitting that here, at the beginning of a series of proverbial instructions, we are introduced to Wisdom herself. Admonition is now leavened by invitation—a pleasure principle. Wisdom enters upon the scene inviting the learner to eat at her table, and making promises and warnings which carry on the idea of personal initiative and judgement begun in vv. 8–19. The search for wisdom is an option; one can accept or refuse. In effect these verses are an educational poem which personifies wisdom who seeks union with mankind. The personalized approach makes the admonition more intimate and even more attractive. The fact that her invitation is given "in the street, in the markets" emphasizes the fact that the pursuit of wisdom is a human, everyday affair, affecting mankind at the level of life. What we have here is simply wisdom teaching personified, but it is possibly a preparation for the later personification of wisdom as divine attribute.

Wisdom's speech reveals an ordered world that maintains itself by its own efforts—good or evil follow naturally from human action, so the young (v. 22) must acquire strength of character. What is important is that this is an *invitation,* not an instruction by parent or teacher. In a less authoritarian age wisdom takes up the teaching mandate of priest and prophet, often indeed using the self-same authority, an appeal to the *Tôrah* (chapters 2—3). Lady Wisdom makes her first, personalized appeal to susceptible youth: acquire good sense and be ruled by it; to do otherwise is supreme folly. If you do not grasp the opportunity when it is offered, you will not get it again. Here we are in the realm of personal morality, human, indeed, but allied to the divine. In vv. 28–30 the religious dimension is revealed: to "hate knowledge" is equated with a refusal to "fear the Lord". Acceptance of this religious principle ensures security for the learner and the "simple", and in that security they can grow. Again, the emphasis is on the inner dimension of human acts—moral good (or bad) resides in a person's interior attitude; the act is merely the external manifestation of one's integrity (vv. 31–32). Evil results from a wicked personality, as naturally as sickness results from eating bad fruit. A balanced relationship to Yahweh combined with an openness to life and a willingness to learn from it is essential if one is to become wise (v. 33).

CHAPTER 2

Already in this second discourse of chapter two the ambient has subtly changed. It is still an invitation to seek wisdom, but now this is more than a merely human quality: the search for wisdom has become a search for a moral and religious quality. Wisdom is related to knowledge of God, and this demands a practical way of life, an ethical response. Technically, the whole chapter is very carefully constructed so as to constitute a formal course of wisdom, in which the passage from pursuit of wisdom to religious understanding and moral commitment is carefully traced. The first four verses are conditional, marking this as the only discourse in the book to begin with a protasis, and they show the prerequisites of the sapiential quest. Wisdom is now a gift of God, granted to those who, by discipline, have searched for it. Thus it presents a challenge: the reader is offered life; is shown the way to it, and is free to accept or reject "discipline".

WISDOM AND KNOWLEDGE OF GOD. 2:1–11.

2 My son, if you receive my words
and treasure up my
commandments with you,
[2]making your ear attentive to wisdom
and inclining your heart to

understanding;
[3]yes, if you cry out for insight
and raise your voice for
understanding,
[4]if you seek it like silver
and search for it as for hidden
treasures;
[5]then you will understand the fear of
the LORD
and find the knowledge of God.
[6]For the LORD gives wisdom;
from his mouth come knowledge
and understanding;
[7]he stores up sound wisdom for the
upright;
he is a shield to those who walk
in integrity,
[8]guarding the paths of justice
and preserving the way of his saints.
[9]Then you will understand
righteousness and justice
and equity, every good path;
[10] for wisdom will come into your heart,
and knowledge will be pleasant to
your soul;
[11] discretion will watch over you;
understanding will guard you;

In classical sapiential fashion this discourse begins with the authority of the teacher, and the obedience and discipline called for in the pupil. But already there is an interesting deviation from the norm. Here the teaching authority is based, not on experience, but on "my commandments" (v. 1). The Hebrew term (*miswotay*) is clearly reminiscent of Deut 11:1 and the *Tôrah*. The teaching of the sage has now become a moral category.

What is asked of the reader is, in fact, no more than is asked of any pupil in any subject: keenness, attention, a willingness to learn and a genuine effort, and this serves to emphasize the change of moral climate, for the result of this discipline is surprising: "fear of the Lord", in another of its manifestations (v. 5). The life of the pupil—the intellectual search for wisdom—has become a quest for God. But it is a search, something one has to strive for—"if you seek it" (v. 4), you will find the search begins and ends with God. This intuition gives a new thrust to the intellectual adventure. In the first four verses we find the traditional search for wisdom, understanding and insight, and the vocabulary is that of Old Wisdom, inculcating intellectual maturity. Now the thrust has changed. The phrase "you will understand" makes it clear that a religious motivation is in question. Yahweh, once discovered, becomes the point of departure for a new moral and intellectual search, a voyage of discovery that springs from divine intimacy. Being a quest, it is clearly something dynamic and not a passive attitude: the one who is wise becomes thereby the "righteous", who reflects the justice of God in a human world. The old concept of retribution has taken on a new aspect of spirituality. The reward that the "upright" can now claim as his own is the companionship and protection of God (vv. 7–8).

A suggestion of the covenant tradition, hinted at in v. 1, returns in v. 8: the "saints" (*hasidîm*) are those who are faithful to a covenant relationship. The fruits of discipline and the quest for wisdom are now the religious virtues of righteousness, justice and equity; a life that is in accord with the will of God and the well-being of the community; and a capacity for discerning that divine will. There follows an openness to further growth and to human fulfillment. From knowledge and fear of God comes the gift of wisdom, and here begins the third step, for wisdom is effective in preserving the moral life of the pupil and keeping him on the path of righteousness.

Verse 9 established the context of moral perception, v. 11 now takes this up and defines it. "Discretion" is a moral gift, including both human good sense and judgement (Old Wisdom) and an insight that derives from communion with God (Later Wisdom). The one so endowed with wisdom can avoid the pitfalls of life, and can discern the true human values and integrate them with religious commitment. In four steps this section has presented a synthesis of the sapiential intention that lies behind Book I. First the teacher's moral credentials are presented, then the pupil's commitment to discipline and the search for wisdom, from which comes knowledge and fear of God; this is the source of wisdom, which in its turn is the source of uprightness of life. This concept of morality is now illustrated by two negative examples, and a return to a positive statement on the "upright".

NEGATIVE: THE PERVERSE MAN. 2:12–15.

[12]delivering you from the way of evil,
from men of perverted speech,
[13]who forsake the paths of uprightness
to walk in the ways of darkness,
[14]who rejoice in doing evil
and delight in the perverseness of evil;
[15]men whose paths are crooked,
and who are devious in their ways.

Along with the next section, these verses form a diptych which gives a negative description of the "wise". The key to the understanding of both is probably v. 9, which seems to determine all that follows. What is achieved by the gift of "understanding" found there? The one who has received the gift of wisdom can discern righteousness, rejoices in familiarity with God, and is preserved by him from the influence of those who speak and do evil. We meet these latter in vv. 12–15.

The vignette presented here is a deliberate parody, carefully constructed, chiastic in form (a b b a), vv. 12–13 being parallel to vv. 14–15. "Men of perverted speech" is unusually strong for Proverbs. The Hebrew word, *tahpukôt*, derives from a root that suggests turning something upside-down. This is a person whose words and actions show him to be devious, naturally a parody of the "upright" of vv. 7b–11. His qualities are negative; he perverts the right order of things and turns the divine order wrong way around. The upright is a positive influence on his environment and contributes to Yahweh's purpose for the world. In like manner the "perverse" man, who lacks moral discernment and follows a twisted path, is a negative influence. Not alone *is* he perverse, he *perverts* others. So the dynamic character of morality is stressed here, just as it was in vv. 1–11. The type of person we meet in vv. 12–15 not only turn aside themselves, they cause others to lose the way. What is emphasized, therefore, is less the character of the morally evil person than the influence that a perverse person, lacking wisdom, has on a community. Being perverse "of speech", he overturns the divine order; being a creature of darkness himself (v. 13), he darkens the path of others (v. 14).

NEGATIVE: THE STRANGE WOMAN. 2:16–19.

[16]You will be saved from the strange woman,
the foreign woman of seductive speech;
[17]she who forsakes the friend of her youth,
forgetting the covenant
she made with her God.
[18]Her house leads down to death,
and her paths to the shades;
[19]None who goes to her returns,
nor regains the paths of life.

(*translation by the author*)

This is a more important vignette than the previous one, for the female motif runs right through chapters 1–9, and is obviously of primary importance to the theological development of the section (cf. 5:3, 20; 6:24; 7:4–5). Indeed, it is used too often in this introduction, and too intuitively, to be taken at its literal level of sexual activity. It can scarcely be a simple matter of adultery; more likely it stands as an image of a particular lifestyle, with the contrast of a good marriage with its fruitfulness and the ecstasy of love, and the wastefulness of prostitution. In the context of Prov 2, it is associated with wisdom as a way of life, as a value in life.

As it stands in the text the image has two possible functions: it may be taken in a literal sense as a warning against adultery, or it can be taken in a transferred sense. Whichever way one sees it, one must remember that this "woman" re-occurs frequently in the next few chapters, so this text should be interpreted in that evolving context. The first thing to remember is that the function of wisdom in this chapter is religious, the "fear of Yahweh" (v. 5), so the woman here is a negative of religion. Next, the covenant relationship suggested by v. 1 and v. 9 inserts the reader into the tradition of the relationship of intimacy between Israel and Yahweh, her "marriage" to God. Allied to the hint of sexual aberration in v. 17, a classic image of religious compromise in the Old Testament (see Hos 1—3 and Jer 1—4), it would appear that we are in the context of religious and sapiential morality.

Since v. 5 deals with the perception of God that is the fruit of the wisdom-search, it may be that the "woman" of vv. 16–19 plays the same role as the "man" of vv. 12–15: she is a perversion of the "wise". In the first place she is that form of stupidity that refuses to recognize true wisdom, and in the second place the "strange" or alien way of life that reflects the perversion from the "way". Certainly, the image is lifelike, realistic. A woman far from her own people and her own religious traditions, she feels she can do what she likes, experience the sweets of life; who is there to dissent? But non-conformism is not necessarily a virtue, it can make one an outsider to one's own. Yet defiance of social conformity can render one very attractive to the unformed young, and a potent temptation to fashionable if not moral ways. Both these aspects of the problem are possible in the text, but the nucleus seems to be v. 17. Many commentators translate this as "the covenant with her husband", but the Hebrew text (using *'elohîm*) can as easily be understood as referring to a covenant with God (*'elohîm*). Text and context make this more likely.

What results is a theology constructed on two levels, with a definite catechetical purpose. The literal meaning presents a woman who has deserted her husband, the "friend of her youth"; but v. 17b allows us to interpret the whole in theological terms, the relationship between Yahweh and those who belong to him. Thus the perversion in question here is the betrayal of the relationship established between God and his "wise" (vv. 7b–11), and the "marriage bond" that is communion between God and his "saints" (v. 8). In fact, Prov 5:15–19 shows that this is not alien to the thought of Book I of Proverbs. As the text stands in the final redaction both concepts, literal and symbolic, seem to be joined. On one hand we find an elevated concept of marriage, love and fidelity that is characteristic of the sapiential tradition; on the other we have a symbolic presentation of the fruits of wisdom, the relationship between the "wise" and Yahweh. The image of "death" in v. 18 confirms this. While it maintains much of its literal sense—in wisdom literature the loss of God is tantamount to a death of all that is truly "human" (1:32)—to a greater degree it signifies spiritual death.

THE RIGHTEOUS ONE. 2:20–22.

[20]So you shall walk in the way of goodness,
and hold fast to the path of the righteous.
[21]For the upright shall possess the land,
and those who maintain integrity remain in it.
[22]But the wicked shall be cut off from the land,
and the treacherous torn away from it.

(*translation by the author*)

Schematically an inclusion, this verse returns the reader to the introductory statement of v. 1. Like that, it is probably a re-statement of the Deuteronomic promise of a prosperity conditional upon religious observance. As in the first section of this chapter, what we have here is a sapiential re-interpretation of the challenge of the *Tôrah*. The language itself is clearly reminiscent of the "covenant blessings" of Deut 11:13, 4:1 and 5:16, and re-inserts us into the positive context of the "wise". Unlike vv. 1–4, however, here the motive for observance of the discipline of the sages has been changed; it remains secular, and reminiscent of Old Wisdom, but it nonetheless achieves a religious end, as Later Wisdom. Those who seek wisdom, and arrive at a more intense awareness of Yahweh, are guided on their journey along the "path of righteousness" (v. 20). In this last portrait of the "wise" the editors of Proverbs present a poetic re-statement of the basic religious option that faith is by definition: "today, choose life or death", wisdom or alienation—*but choose*!

CHAPTER 3

This chapter more firmly identifies wisdom with religion, the "wise" enjoying a rich and intimate relationship with God. The whole chapter is marked with the vocabulary of *Tôrah* religion: "law" and "commandments", one divine, the other more human. The central intuition of the chapter derives from this human-divine intimacy, purely human activity being seen now as in some way also divine activity. This sanctification of human effort shows the influence of the Priestly tradition.

THE WAYS OF HUMAN MORALITY. 3:1–10.

3 My son, do not forget my teaching,
but let your heart keep my
commandments;
[2]for length of days and years of life
and abundant welfare will they
give you.
[3]Let not loyalty and faithfulness
forsake you;
bind them about your neck,
write them on the tablet of your
heart.
[4]So you will find favor and good
repute

in the sight of God and man.
[5]Trust in the LORD with all your heart,
and do not rely on your own
insight.
[6]In all your ways acknowledge him,
and he will make straight your
paths.
[7]Be not wise in your own eyes;
fear the LORD, and turn away from
evil.
[8]It will be healing to your flesh
and refreshment to your bones.
[9]Honour the LORD with your substance
and with the first fruits of all your
produce;
[10]then your barns will be filled with
plenty,
and your vats will be bursting
with wine.

This pericope introduces a purely yahwistic tone to the sapiential concept of "discipline", a dimension of mutual influence between secular and religious life. Taking up the tone of 2:22 the sage calls for attention, shows the consequences, and arrives at religious wisdom, a process that is analogous and complementary to the second discourse. There is a transition from direct parent/teacher authority in v. 1 to direct divine authority in v. 5, the core of yahwistic faith. Verse 2 is covenant terminology, and may be a reference to the New Covenant theology of individual responsibility, and the need for a personal commitment to life and wisdom. This is a development of the basic theme stressed in 1:7, "fear of the Lord". "Let not loyalty forsake you", the injunction of v. 3, introduces a double theme: human action and its consequences. The terms "loyalty" and "faithfulness" designate the distinctive quality of the religious man in his relationship to God, and is central to the theology of Proverbs. They are human virtues, that mark the intimate nature of the human being, most often found in such entrance liturgies as Ps 15 (14) and Ps 24 (23). What is in question is an interior quality that results in a certain external way of life in relation to society and to the world. They therefore prepare the pupil for encounter with the divine. Clearly, these verses present a theological re-interpretation of the wisdom instruction as one passes from the tutelage of the sage to that of God. The first fruit of wisdom is a mutual relationship between the pupil and God, faithfulness and goodness, the virtues that reflect human love, and therefore a personal relationship of intimacy that is emphasized by "your heart" in v. 3b, and the consequences of seeking wisdom in v. 4. The fulfillment depicted here is an affirmation of human values. "Trusting in the Lord" in v. 5 suggests an interior dedication to God as wisdom becomes religious illumination rather than human education. Understanding must be based on grace, the divine illumination that comes from knowledge of God, and it is this that guarantees to keep the pupil on the right path. These two verses (5–6) serve to remind us of the interior dimension of covenant religion, the mutual love of God and man.

On this basis is introduced once more the doctrine of the two ways of wisdom ethics. One can walk in the path of life only when one recognizes God in that path. Three times in Prov 1—9 human happiness is due to God, here and in v. 32 and later on in 5:21. Otherwise in Proverbs reward and punishment is meted out on the basis of a universal law of retribution. In fact, the picture we get of God is of an administrator who hands out to man precisely what he has earned by his conformity to rules. In vv. 7–10 we see another dimension to "fear of God"—it has now become a source of moral and physical good. This morality is manifestly influenced by the cultic requirements of the covenant. It is clearly this interleaving of "secular" and "religious" in the makeup of a "wise" person that marks the theology of the book, bringing a sense of human totality and wholeness. Moral good is fleshed out with material sufficiency. In Deut 26 and 28 we find the probable source for vv. 9–10, the precept of offering the first fruits to Yahweh. In these verses, however, the formulation is changed, the offering becoming a spiritual offering. This suggests that this section of Prov 3 offers a combination of traditional "legal" religion, and a newer, sapiential, tradition of personal and very human love between mankind and God more proper to the prophets. The vital dynamic of human life is "trust in the Lord" (v. 5), in the context of daily life and the search for truth. This dynamic regulates life, its ideals, its inspiration.

A HYMN TO WISDOM. 3:11–18.

[11]My son, do not despise the LORD'S
discipline
or be weary of his reproof,
[12]for the LORD reproves him whom he
loves,
as a father the son in whom he
delights.
[13]Happy is the man who finds wisdom,
and the man who gets
understanding,
[14]for the gain from it is better than
gain from silver
and its profit better than gold.
[15]She is more precious than jewels,
and nothing you desire can compare
with her.
[16]Long life is in her right hand;
in her left hand are riches and
honour.
[17]Her ways are ways of pleasantness,
and all her paths are peace.
[18]She is a tree of life to those who lay
hold of her;
those who hold her fast are called
happy.

The reward of the wise is not to be taken in a simplistic sense, as this section makes clear. Justice is not necessarily associated with "prosperity" in a material sense, nor can it easily be measured. The sages recognized the sinful nature of the human being, a creature always in need of purification. The price one pays for the relationship with God revealed in the previous section is an attitude of docility, a willingness to learn and to accept the discipline of the Lord's healing reproof. Experience shows that prosperity is not always the lot of the "wise" or the righteous, at least in any obvious sense. So the inequity of life remains a problem, and is recognized as one. The truly wise remains patient in adversity, and accepts whatever comes his way. Here in Prov 3 suffering is seen as a paternal discipline, a form of divine instruction analogous to the parental rod or the teacher's cane. But the emphasis is more positive than might appear—for the paternal love of Yahweh endures even in suffering; it is a present dynamic that leavens human life.

There follows a hymn to Wisdom, a development of the sapiential theme of the true meaning of "prosperity", which is less material wealth than the abundance of life and happiness that wisdom brings. The structure of this passage is more homogeneous, being the "beatitude" form of the sapiential tradition. The presentation here of wisdom personified serves to personalize the message of vv. 1–12; the benefits of companionship with wisdom accrue from the *Tôrah* and the commandments of God, as do the benefits of wisdom in the first part. What Wisdom offers is life in its fullness—qualitatively, self-fulfillment and honour; quantitatively, longevity. Material wealth is promised, but is secondary to the possession of Wisdom herself. Here we meet two types of persons: the "get rich quick" category, and those who seek first the permanent values, and receive wealth as a bonus or added gift. Two images serve to communicate the idea of "life" in all its richness—"peace" and the "tree of life". Peace, *shalôm,* is the fullness of human well-being, material and spiritual. It is a totally rich life in the land. The concept of "tree of life'' takes us back to Genesis and the origins of mankind and the human condition. There it represented mankind's search for a knowledge to which only God had a right. Much of the biblical tradition took it in this sense, adopting an attitude that discouraged man from a cultural and intellectual quest (as Ezek 28; Isa 10 and 14). In comparing wisdom with the tree of life Prov 3:18 may perhaps be making a statement that equates wisdom and the sapiential endeavour with a return to the sources, and to the ideal of perfect man before the fall. Through wisdom, humanity can return once more to the lost garden of paradise. Thus the fruit of wisdom is twofold, longevity and a certain material well-being, and an interior quality in life itself. What otherwise in the biblical tradition is the fruit of covenant observance.

WISDOM'S CREATIVE FUNCTION. 3:19–20.

> [19]The LORD by wisdom founded the earth;
> by understanding he established the heavens;
> [20]by his knowledge the deeps broke forth,
> and the clouds drop down the dew.

Wisdom is the most precious possession, bringing joy, longevity, human fulfillment. But it is more than that. It has a transcendent value, functioning with Yahweh in the ongoing creativity he exercises in the world. This section of the text of Prov 3 presents the creative power of God, and Wisdom is associated with him in the act of creation. The transcendent value of wisdom (later taken up more fully in chapter 8) is dominant here. These two verses are reminiscent of the Priestly tradition, the cosmological overtones being those of Gen 1 and the language (particularly of v. 20) reminding one of Gen 7:11, a priestly insertion. The context of Prov 3:19–20 remains that of the reader's search for wisdom. Thus the text sets out to clarify the learner's relationship to God by analogy with Wisdom's relationship to Yahweh in the act of creation (an idea that is taken up again in 8:22). Theologically, what results is a smooth integration of learning, human knowledge, and religion. Human wisdom must be, by its nature, a share in the divine wisdom. Mankind thus holds its own destiny in its own hands: man confronts life, acts as he sees fit (v. 21), and everything else, be it good or bad, fruitful or not, follows naturally. Creation theology presents many laws, but the only law of wisdom is that imposed by existence itself, and humanity's search for meaning.

MATURITY IS THE FRUIT OF WISDOM. 3:21–35.

[21]My son, keep sound wisdom and discretion;
let them not escape from your sight,
[22]and they will be life for your soul
and adornment for your neck.
[23]Then you will walk on your way securely
and your foot will not stumble.
[24]If you sit down, you will not be afraid;
when you lie down, your sleep will be sweet.
[25]Do not be afraid of sudden panic,
or of the ruin of the wicked, when it comes;
[26]for the LORD will be your confidence
and will keep your foot from being caught.
[27]Do not withhold good from those to whom it is due,
when it is in your power to do it.

[28]Do not say to your neighbour, "Go,
and come again,
tomorrow I will give it"—when
you have it with you.
[29]Do not plan evil against your
neighbour
who dwells trustingly beside you.
[30]Do not contend with a man for no
reason,
when he has done you no harm.
[31]Do not envy a man of violence
and do not choose any of his
ways;
[32]for the perverse man is an
abomination to the LORD,
but the upright are in his confidence.
[33]The LORD'S curse is on the house of
the wicked,
but he blesses the abode of the
righteous.
[34]Toward the scorners he is scornful,
but to the humble he shows
favour.
[35]The wise will inherit honour,
but fools get disgrace.

What wisdom effects comes both from human effort and as a gift of God. Given that perception, v. 26 may be seen as the high point of this final section of chapter 3. The continuing metaphor of "the way" (vv. 23–24) shows the moral preoccupation throughout. The first verses present a concept of worldly maturity, the human virtues of prudence and perception, to which v. 26 adds a religious colouring. Through these human and divine qualities God works to bring the hearer to maturity. "They will be life for your soul" (v. 22) refers to terrestrial life, material existence as it is experienced. The grace of wisdom is more than an ornament; it is a state of well-being, as the parallel structure of 22a/22b brings out. The notion of reward here, in concert with the notion of retribution in vv. 16–17, is a return to the traditional doctrine of retribution found in Deuteronomy, and it is possible that the author has recourse to it as a form of insurance: he has postulated a daring relationship of intimacy between the truly wise and God (vv. 1–10 and 19–20); now he safeguards this by a return to conventional ideas. "Do not be afraid" (v. 25) is used in a theological sense, and is the only occurrence of this negative form of "fear" in the sapiential literature. Its primary meaning is reassurance of consolation, and it is spoken by a teacher who has divine authority for what he says. The encouragement is positive, aimed towards concrete social situations and is older in style than the preceding verses. Verses 27–29 are concerned with the practical task of living in society, and inculcates the virtues needed to live with others. This is then paralleled by vv. 30–32. Two types are opposed, the upright and the perverse, and both are viewed in the context of the community. Betraying the trust of a neighbour (28–29) is more than a social crime, it is the betrayal of the relationship of trust that allows one to stand before God. Social and religious attitudes are at one. Lack of positive generosity in whatever it is you do reflects a smallness of mind that vitiates any possibility of truly human commerce; the emphasis is on vv. 27b and 28b: "when it is in your power . . . when you have it with you". One does not take a measuring rod to generosity. The final verses of the section introduce the religious aspect of human conduct once more. Equivocation, in speech or in deed, is ultimately an offence against God, whereas the person of integrity carries weight in the community and has a natural dignity. This precept of human love is also one of religious love—an idea taken up elsewhere in the tradition by Sir 4:1–6. It is somewhat strange an idea in the context of the Old Testament, but perhaps one can see here at least in embryo the later concept of the mutual love of human beings standing for the love of God for mankind.

Fear of Yahweh has already been presented as a religious humanism. In this section of the text one can find one element of this humanism—normal friendship; an effort at giving human relationships a divine dimension. God's love for us is a blueprint for our attitude to others. Secular life is no more than an extension of the divine.

CHAPTER 4

The teacher's instruction now takes a new form, as Chapter 4 presents three warnings, couched in affective language, designed to appeal not only to the intellect but to the emotions of a favourite pupil. The way of righteousness is not only good, it is pleasurable; though difficult at times, it affords a sense of achievement. Let the reader only pay attention, and personal fulfillment will be gained by it.

WISDOM AS LOVER AND SPOUSE. 4:1–9.

4 Hear, O sons, a father's instruction,
and be attentive, that you may
gain insight;
[2]for I give you good precepts:
do not forsake my teaching.
[3]When I was a son with my father,
tender, the only one in the sight
of my mother,
[4]he taught me, and said to me,
"Let your heart hold fast my words;
keep my commandments, and live;
[5]do not forget, and do not turn away
from the words of my mouth.
Get wisdom; get insight.

[6]Do not forsake her, and she will
keep you;
love her, and she will guard you.
[7]The beginning of wisdom is this:
Get wisdom,
and whatever you get, get insight.
[8]Prize her highly, and she will exalt
you;
she will honour you if you embrace
her.
[9]She will place on your head a fair
garland;
she will bestow on you a beautiful
crown."

Formal instruction gives way to impassioned plea in this first of the three warnings, still couched in the parent/pupil style, still calling for respect and docility as the primary attitude. The tone is familiar, intimate and personal, reflecting a preoccupation that is dear to proverbial literature: the centrality of the home in passing on the traditions that make life liveable. In the whole of the first book there is no clear distinction between formal and family education, as it is never clear whether teacher or parent speaks. Whichever it is here, the affectionate family tone predominates and gives the teaching a new poignancy. Youth must remain open to guidance, and to new ideas, for it is thus that one inserts oneself into one's traditions. So here we meet a teacher anxious to pass on the fruits of a lifetime's experience, and the most basic advice of all is "get wisdom; get insight!" (v. 5), an emotion-charged imperative. The sage addresses first of all the "heart" (4b), seat of human vitality; and the pupil is encouraged to search for wisdom as one would search for a life's companion. If this involves sacrifice, and indeed it will, count it well made. Once acquired, wisdom will be a joy forever, only bind it to yourself by fidelity, care and love. The teacher has clearly found wisdom for himself, and seeks to draw the heart of the pupil to share the same joy: "do not turn away from the words of my mouth".

Manifestly, what is in question is the wisdom that the sage acquired in the home. It is not just a question of accepting parental traditions, but education in depth, steeping oneself in a learning that furnishes a way of life. Wisdom is the first priority, and she is presented as a feminine vehicle of spirituality through which Yahweh presents himself to men. It is possible that this concept stands for a quasi-mystical union, analogous to sexual attraction. One must have a true source for human life and love, and wisdom so perceived furnishes the values and priorities that stand one in good stead. But it must become part of one's very being, an internal principle to be maintained by devotion. The personification of wisdom as lover and bride may be a reaction to the "strange woman" of 2:16. If so, the moral dimension is predominant, and the marital aspect of the life of learning. Wisdom so gained will indeed be a faithful, and fruitful, spouse—as long as the personal adherence remains strong, she will be the dominant factor in one's life.

MORALITY AS AN OPTION. 4:10–19.

[10]Hear, my son, and accept my words,
that the years of your life may be many.
[11]I have taught you the way of wisdom;
I have led you in the paths of uprightness.
[12]When you walk, your step will not be hampered;
and if you run, you will not stumble.
[13]Keep hold of instruction, do not let go;
guard her, for she is your life.
[14]Do not enter the path of the wicked,
and do not walk in the way of

evil men.
[15]Avoid it; do not go on it;
turn away from it and pass on.
[16]For they cannot sleep unless they
have done wrong;
they are robbed of sleep unless
they have made some one
stumble.
[17]For they eat the bread of wickedness
and drink the wine of violence.
[18]But the path of the righteous is like
the light of dawn,
which shines brighter and brighter
until full day.
[19]The way of the wicked is like deep
darkness;
they do not know over what they
stumble.

The personal touch is maintained in this presentation of the classic "two ways" of morality, the way of the righteous and that of the wicked, and it strengthens the element of *choice* that is now introduced. Here we have a personalization of the challenge of the *Tôrah:* "I set before you this day life . . . and death, now choose" (Deut 30:15). In Deuteronomy, "way" is an option of obedience and of future commitment; in Proverbs it is an ongoing experience of life and conduct. So wisdom is essentially a way of life, and a vital call that shapes life. Verse 11 sets out her function, to teach one to "walk" actively in a given "way" (option). One aspect of the discipline this entails is to avoid the "ways of the wicked" (v. 14), a constant theme in sapiential literature, seen already in Prov 1:10–19; 2:12–15; and in an extended image in Ps 1. Here in Prov 3 the emphasis is on the influences that can ruin one's life and weaken one's resolve to walk steadily in a world that the parent and teacher knows is antipathetic. The "bread of wickedness" (v. 17) is a drug that enslaves those foolish enough to eat it, and inevitably becomes, not just a pleasure, but a craving. Conversely, the way of wisdom is compared to the "light of dawn" (v. 18), with the religious connotation that always accompanies the image of light in the wisdom tradition. To see light is to live fully, a mode of existence totally opposed to sin. It implies a positive ethical choice, while darkness (v. 19), equally possible as a choice, involves walking a path that is devious and tortuous, the way of lost souls. Here is the text of vv. 10–19 the "righteous" are those who have made a definite choice, and have persisted in the discipline that is required to maintain the sometimes difficult consequences of that choice.

EXHORTATION. 4:20–27.

[20]My son, be attentive to my words;
incline your ear to my sayings.
[21]Let them not escape from your sight;
keep them within your heart.
[22]For they are life to him who finds them,
and healing to all his flesh.
[23]Keep your heart with all vigilance;
for from it flow the springs of life.
[24]Put away from you crooked speech,
and put devious talk far from you.
[25]Let your eyes look directly forward,
and your gaze be straight before you.
[26]Take heed to the path of your feet,
then all your ways will be sure.
[27]Do not swerve to the right or to the left;
turn your foot away from evil.

The final exhortation in this chapter is dominated by the theme of vigilance, and establishes the keeping of one's heart and eyes as the principle of morality. This is practical morality, based on experience. As always, the first requirement is to learn the implications of the good life, and to implement them seriously. Once again (as in the previous chapter) we are in the context of the entrance liturgies and their demand for interiority in religion. To "guard one's heart" is essential. One sets up the interior quality of personal integrity, and from this flows truthful speech, honest dealing in thought and action. What one *does* then is seen to be the articulation of what one *is*.

The words of the sage, and his instructions, are "life and healing" (v. 22), and it is this idea that dominates the exhortation. In this context "life" comprises all earthly blessings, and the parallel "healing" is preservation from all the evils that beset this terrestrial existence. The listing of vital organs, that follows in vv. 23–25, shows the all-inclusive nature of discipline. One must take adequate care over the path one seeks to follow; preparing it carefully, seeing to the removal of all obstacles, eliminating any need of detour. The image is familiar, taken from the contemporary custom of preparing a king's or an envoy's path (see for example Isa 40:1–4), so that no departure from the direct route is necessary, and the journey is expedited. With precisely the same care and effort must one facilitate one's own journey through life by strict attention to instruction and by unswerving self-discipline. The end of the journey makes the effort worth while—it is no less than life in its fullness.

CHAPTER 5

The discourse of chapter 5 unfolds like a very carefully limned diptych, with two matching sections, each in itself being a unity.

vv. 1–14:		**vv. 15–23:**	
1– 6:	"loose woman"	15–19:	good wife
7–11:	avoid her	20:	"loose woman"
12–14:	moral conclusion (secular)	21–23:	moral conclusion (religious)

The two dominant ideas, the loose woman and the good wife, are themes of the good way of life very dear to the author of Prov 1—9. The whole forms an elongated metaphor for ethical conduct deriving from an affective motivation.

THE LOOSE WOMAN. 5:1–14.

5 My son, be attentive to my wisdom,
incline your ear to my
understanding;
[2]that you may keep discretion,
and your lips may guard knowledge.
[3]For the lips of a loose woman drip
honey,

and her speech is smoother than
oil;
[4]but in the end she is bitter as
wormwood,
sharp as a two-edged sword.
[5]Her feet go down to death;
her steps follow the path to Sheol;
[6]she does not take heed to the path
of life;
her ways wander, and she does not
know it.
[7]And now, O sons, listen to me,
and do not depart from the words
of my mouth.
[8]Keep your way far from her,
and do not go near the door of
her house;
[9]lest you give your honour to others
and your years to the merciless;
[10] lest strangers take their fill of your
strength,
and your labours go to the house
of an alien;
[11] and at the end of your life you groan,
when your flesh and body are
consumed,
[12] and you say, "How I hated discipline,
and my heart despised reproof!
[13] I did not listen to the voice of my
teachers
or incline my ear to my instructors.
[14] I was at the point of utter ruin
in the assembled congregation."

Here we have a second warning against the "strange woman" (cf. 2:16), and as usual it begins suddenly, with no warning. The introduction (1–2) hardly seems related to what follows, but in fact it reiterates the basic sapiential programmatic: openness of mind is an essential attitude in the search for learning. Then vv. 3–6 introduce the main topic, which is hammered home by the emphatic clauses in vv. 9 and 10—"lest . . ." in Hebrew *pen*. The context is the quest for wisdom and understanding; once acquired, these should be a person's defence and protection in facing up to life in the world. This is part of a sequence of thought that can be traced back to Prov 1. This first discourse is strongly influenced by the vocabulary of Later Wisdom and traditional morality, and here personified Wisdom is introduced. Prov 2 adds a taste of prophetic imagery to the picture, by drawing a parallel between infidelity to Yahweh, and "adultery" with a "strange" or foreign woman. Chapter 5 is more practical in its aim than previous discourses, dealing with a life situation of marriage and fidelity, in the normal run of things the natural way of life that awaits every pupil.

What Prov 5 achieves is a remarkable integration of the secular and the religious, and a realism that is unusual in these introductory chapters. The actuality of human love, marriage and fidelity is what is in question, but on a secondary level this becomes an analogy with one's natural relationship to Yahweh. Conversely, then, this *religious* aspect of love can become the basis for our understanding of human love. The process is classically sapiential, beginning with what one can experience, in this case human sexuality; this supplies the language by which one can arrive at a perception of God's love; and this in its turn helps one find the deeper significance of human love and fidelity.

On the practical level of the text, this section presents a warning against adultery, repugnant to the sages not only because it was a real temptation, especially to youth, which could destroy one's own marriage, but also because it destroyed another person's marriage relationship. It was a most disruptive force in society. Thus the *literal* level is obvious. But it is not really the custom of the sages to give so much emphasis to this aspect of immorality, nor is it the wisdom style to rest a case there, without using it as a symbol of something that has more universal meaning. The "loose woman" of v. 3, in Hebrew *zarâ*, is personified seduction. She leads a fevered life, and, herself lacking stability, she unseats others. The image, which is clearly that of sexual love, is also found in the Old Testament for the love of God, as in Ps 19 (18), and Ps 119 (118). In the following verses we pass from image to reality. The emphasis is less on the wickedness of adultery in itself than on the susceptibility of youth faced with influences it cannot fully cope with. As long as the pupil lacks wisdom, he remains a prey to the dangers of life, and is wide open to exploitation by "the merciless" (v. 9). So the pupil is warned to shun temptation: life can be full and fruitful, and one passes this way but once, so do not waste life's potential. In any case, there are also the practical implications to be faced: the "merciless" who will consume "your years"—the offended husband and family, the regrets and personal recriminations that will follow you down the years, the growing awareness of the contempt of the community.

In this first section, clearly secular in its tone, there is no condemnation of sex, but rather a positive recognition of the pleasure of sex and a respect for it. But the teaching is clear-eyed and practical. The human sex-drive is potent, not always easy to control, and this is particularly true of susceptible youth with fire in its veins. So it is essential first to inculcate a positive attitude on the part of the young, then a personal discipline, and a perception that can recognize and avoid the wrong circumstances.

THE GOOD WIFE. 5:15–23.

[15]Drink water from your own cistern,
flowing water from your own well.
[16]Should your springs be scattered
abroad,
streams of water in the streets?
[17]Let them be for yourself alone,
and not for strangers with you.
[18]Let your fountain be blessed,
and rejoice in the wife of your
youth,

[19] a lovely hind, a graceful doe.
Let her affection fill you at all times
with delight,
be infatuated always with her love.
[20]Why should you be infatuated, my
son, with a loose woman
and embrace the bosom of an
adventuress?
[21]For a man's ways are before the eyes
of the LORD,
and he watches all his paths.
[22]The iniquities of the wicked ensnare
him,
and he is caught in the toils of his sin.
[23]He dies for lack of discipline,
and because of his great folly he
is lost.

This short, didactic passage on fidelity and happiness in marriage presents the obverse of the coin. Such a change in imagery within an instruction serves a pedagogic function. It sharpens the attention and the emotional involvement *of the reader.* Thus it calls for an affective as well as an intellectual response. The first principle (vv. 1–14) was an appeal to good sense, now the emotions are being involved.

Fidelity in a monogamous marriage is inculcated, as is clear from v. 15, for the unity and strength of the family, and ultimately of society, depend on it. Thus marriage and the home are thought to be the only acceptable context for sexual intercourse. But interestingly enough, the vocabulary of v. 15 suggests that this is not the primary motive for fidelity. Two verses, 15 and 20, form a minor inclusion within the section, and the terminology is striking: "water", "a lovely hind, a graceful doe", "be infatuated with her love"; all of this is imagery that is more common to erotic love poetry, such as the Song of Songs, than to an academic instruction like Proverbs. For example, this language re-echoes in Cant 2:7, 9, 17; 3:5; 4:5, 12–15; 7:4; etc. It appears that in Proverbs also marriage comes to be described in sexual terms, and the beauty of the wife is equally sensual in its presentation (v. 19). In the Old Testament sexuality is seen as an imperative of nature, a created good and therefore a category that has its own interest for theology. Children are indeed a blessing, but they are not considered the only reason for sex. Predominant in these texts is an awareness of the human richness of the relationship between man and woman. Sex, within the context of marriage, is one of the fruits of the "good life" (v. 15) and is therefore to be desired for itself. The theme of marital fidelity is taken up again in 22:14; 23:27 and 30:20.

In dealing with young people—a preoccupation of Prov 1—9—the greatest danger is the tendency they show to relax their guard and so be led into actual debauchery. For this reason, among others, the "loose woman" is associated with "Folly". In describing marriage, monogamy is a prime point, being one of the most difficult aspects of that relationship, but the personal joys that intimacy brings are also underlined. In this text we do not have the preoccupation with household administration found later in 31:10. Prov 5 is on a more deeply human level, and this is the basis of the theological development no more than hinted at here (v. 18). As always in chapters 1—9 the context is that of the process of maturity, and in vv. 15-20 only the human aspect is treated: the personal, affective and sentimental dimension. The last verses, 21-23, add the theological preoccupation in a short phrase that sketches God's involvement in all human affairs. The effect of human weakness and vacillation on the way through life is not only of worldly concern to the sages, it is a moral problem also; "death" (v. 23) for want of wisdom is not just material death, it is spiritual. As with all human endeavor, God's is the final sanction.

CHAPTER 6

The sequence of thought is momentarily broken in Chapter 6. In the first part (vv. 1–19) we have four short interpolations made by a sage that deal with the commonplace morality of social life: going surety for a neighbour (1–5), laziness (6–11), scandalmongering (12–15) and hypocrisy (16–19). The whole section is marked by a concern for community well-being, and all of the faults are offences against the social structure. A wise person does not take a pledge, which merely exhibits solidarity with one who does not deserve it, nor does he endanger his domestic peace by going to a money-lender. One does one's job to the best of one's ability, for on such is community built up. Verses 12–15 present the obverse, drawing a savage caricature of a shallow, untrustworthy person who is poison in a community, a trouble-maker and thus a most dangerous leaven in any group. Finally, vv. 16–19 present a numerical "proverb" that sums up the section by emphasizing the need for social balance. The teacher's preoccupation is to form a worthy and constructive member of the community by stressing the mutual relationship and interdependence that must exist between individual and group.

These verses are clearly an insertion that disrupts the context of Prov 1—9, and separates the last verse of chapter 5 from its logical sequel, which follows in 6:20 with a further discourse.

WARNING AGAINST SEXUAL IMMORALITY. 6:20–35.

[20]My son, keep your father's
commandment,
and forsake not your mother's
teaching.
[21]Bind them upon your heart always;
tie them about your neck.
[22]When you walk, they will lead
you;
when you lie down, they will
watch over you;
and when you awake, they will
talk with you.
[23]For the commandment is a lamp and
the teaching a light,
and the reproofs of discipline are
the way of life,
[24]to preserve you from the evil
woman,
from the smooth tongue of the
adventuress.
[25]Do not desire her beauty in your
heart,
and do not let her capture you
with her eyelashes;
[26]for a harlot may be hired for a loaf
of bread,
but an adulteress stalks a man's
very life.
[27]Can a man carry fire in his bosom
and his clothes not be burned?
[28]Or can one walk upon hot coals
and his feet not be scorched?
[29]So is he who goes in to his
neighbour's wife;
none who touches her will go
unpunished.

[30]Do not men despise a thief if he
steals
to satisfy his appetite when he is
hungry?
[31]And if he is caught, he will pay
sevenfold;
he will give all the goods of his
house.
[32]He who commits adultery has no
sense;
he who does it destroys himself.
[33]Wounds and dishonour will he get,
and his disgrace will not be wiped
away.
[34]For jealousy makes a man furious,
and he will not spare when he
takes revenge.
[35]He will accept no compensation,
nor be appeased though you
multiply gifts.

This begins a new discourse that takes up the theme of chapter 5, and, like that, is a teacher/parent admonition. The purpose of the wisdom instruction is "to preserve you from the evil woman" (v. 24), the perverse influence outlined in 5:1–14. Like the earlier instruction in 2:1, the authority of the preceptor is that of the *Tôrah,* both the form and the vocabulary of vv. 20–23 being that of Deuteronomy. Once again the context is that of wisdom instruction that re-interprets for a new age the religious mandate of the Law. In fact, 6:20—7:27 takes the form of a catechesis that aims at enticing a pupil or reader to adhere to the spirit of yahwistic faith, and to the traditions of the people. In a way it is more explicit than the previous discourses, being drawn more obviously from Deut 6, 11 and 13. The law of God is the most precious possession, it must be held close. In particular, 6:20–35 fastens on adultery, possibly the most dangerous of temptations to the young. Once again, v. 22 presents morality in terms of a dynamic of life—it is a path one walks, with the commandments at one's shoulder as a guide on the way; at every stage of life's journey the Law, as propounded by the sage, should be the motive force for human activity.

Of all the human aberrations, sexual indulgence and especially adultery is the most pernicious, because the most mindless. It is a form of self-indulgence, a surrender to the emotions and the lower faculties. The only sure guide is the intellectual perception and moral balance supplied by wisdom—and the terminology of v. 23, which conceives of *Tôrah* in terms of "lamp" (*ner*), and wisdom in terms of "light" (*'ôr*) underline this. In the later period that produced Prov 1—9 both terms are related to the light of divine revelation, and are often synonymous with "life", that is a mature human existence, joyful and fulfilled. In this more obviously theological context, the return of the "evil woman" in v. 24, taking up as it does the thread of 5:20 and 2:16, may equally have a symbolic, rather than a literal, significance: lack of wisdom, an immature religious perception, and so a spiritual debility. Literally a harlot (as v. 26 seems to suggest), she stands for a basic estrangement from Yahweh, the "[covenant] companion of her youth" (5:18 and 2:16). Anyone who contemplates either aberration, literal or moral, may just as well "carry fire in his bosom" (v. 27), the end result will be no different: exclusion from the community (v. 30), a high price to pay (v. 31), and most important of all, forfeiture of the fullness of *shalôm* that is the fruit of wisdom.

CHAPTER 7

The fifth episode in the "pupil's progress", where the fundamental option between wisdom and immaturity is laid bare, presents a psychological drama of temptation with two opposing characters, both seductive—"sister wisdom" and the "adventuress". So it continues the series of personified virtues that began in chapter 1.

THE INVITATION. 7:1–5.

7My son, keep my words
and treasure up my commandments
with you;
[2]keep my commandments and live,
keep my teachings as the apple of
your eye;
[3]bind them on your fingers,
write them on the tablet of your
heart.
[4]Say to wisdom, "You are my sister,"
and call insight your intimate
friend;
[5]to preserve you from the loose
woman,
from the adventuress with her
smooth words.

This pericope is a unit, and continues both the style and the preoccupation of the previous discourses. It has been suggested that it forms an inclusion with vv. 24–27, and if this is so the combination of secular and religious morality still pertains, as it did in earlier discussions of adultery; and so does the temptation proffered by the "strange" woman. It is possibly the last part of an evolving instruction on true wisdom, or intellectual and moral maturity. The formulation of the invitation remains basically the same; "commandments" suggest once again the religious authority of the instructor, and "teachings" reflect the more intimate concern of the teacher for the pupil. Both formal instruction and personal example must shape human life, giving the neophyte a stable centre of balance. It is not merely a question of laws to be observed, but a way of life that is to be assimilated: nothing less deserves the name "wisdom". Given the nature of the human condition a firm set of values is necessary if one is not to lose one's way. Indeed, "and live" (v. 2) is the key-word in the invitation. A quality of life is what is in question, and not merely a temporal existence. "Apple of your eye" takes up again in v. 2 the concept of "light" in chapters 4 and 6. Without light, one is doomed to darkness and subsequent death. Adherence to the sage's instruction is more than a form; a personal commitment is called for and two aspects of wisdom come together here: interiority, and external conformity to a code. This is brought out by the affective note that is sounded in the injunction of v. 4; the bond between student and the discipline of learning is as intimate, and as attractive as that between brother and sister, between the two halves of one's life. The final verse of the introduction (v. 5) adds a new element to the exordium. The attraction of a natural intimacy can strengthen one against the seduction of unnatural vice.

WISDOM IS A CONSCIOUS CHOICE. 7:6–23.

> [6]For at the window of my house
> I have looked out through my

lattice,
[7]and I have seen among the simple,
I have perceived among the youths,
a young man without sense,
[8]passing along the street near her corner,
taking the road to her house
[9]in the twilight, in the evening,
at the time of night and darkness.
[10]And lo, a woman meets him,
dressed as a harlot, wily of heart.
[11]She is loud and wayward,
her feet do not stay at home;
[12]now in the street, now in the market,
and at every corner she lies in wait.
[13]She seizes him and kisses him,
and with impudent face she says to him:
[14]"I had to offer sacrifices,
and today I have paid my vows;
[15]so now I have come out to meet you,
to seek you eagerly, and I have found you.
[16]I have decked my couch with coverings,
coloured spreads of Egyptian linen;
[17]I have perfumed my bed with myrrh,
aloes, and cinnamon.
[18]Come, let us take our fill of love till morning;
let us delight ourselves with love.
[19]For my husband is not at home;
he has gone on a long journey;
[20]he took a bag of money with him;
at full moon he will come home."

[21] With much seductive speech she
persuades him;
with her smooth talk she compels
him.
[22] All at once he follows her,
as an ox goes to the slaughter,
or as a stag is caught fast
[23] till an arrow pierces its entrails;
as a bird rushes into a snare;
he does not know that it will cost
him his life.

The short story now so dramatically presented is meant to capture the heart as well as the mind of the reader. The vivacity with which it is presented suggests that it may well be the sage is speaking from personal experience—once again the victim is an "innocent abroad", acted upon rather than acting, unformed, immature, suggestible. And this is the key, for no-one facing up to life can afford the luxury of being suggestible, this is merely to look for trouble. But it is not a picture without guilt, for the youth makes very little effort to escape—"at once he follows her" (v. 22), and in any case what was he doing "on the road to her house, in the twilight"? Already the moral significance is established. In the sapiential tradition twilight represents the half-world of temptation considered though not yet accepted, that moment when the darkness of night and oblivion overtakes the light of day (Job 5:14; 24:15). The way of wickedness is always a conscious choice.

Again in this pericope, while the literary level is clear, the religious level is dominant. The vocabulary of vv. 14–15 is cultual, so the temptation is presented as a conscious religious choice. Deliberately, the imagery is richly significant, truly a parable. While the basic fault is intellectual adolescence, this in itself is considered culpable, for it is the breeding ground of sin. He quite simply had not gone to the effort of making "wisdom his sister"; he had not acquired a set of values.

NEED FOR A POSITIVE GOAL IN LIFE. 7:24–27.

[24] And now, O sons, listen to me,
and be attentive to the words of
my mouth.
[25] Let not your heart turn aside to her
ways,
do not stray into her paths;
[26] for many a victim has she laid low;
yea, all her slain are a mighty host.
[27] Her house is the way to Sheol,
going down to the chambers of
death.

The conclusion, once again in the form of a wisdom instruction, reintroduces the theme of "the path". Discipline and training are essential if youth is to attain maturity and succeed in avoiding the path to perdition. Verse 27 presents an image that sustains the theme of option underlined in the central illustration of temptation. "Her house is the way to Sheol" may have been taken from the Akkadian story of the *Descent of Ishtar to the Netherworld.* There are many paths that lead through life, and one of these leads through the house of the adulteress straight to the bowels of death. But one must set one's feet on this path, and one must keep to it, for the alternative of the paths of life are also possible. The teacher places the reader in the same situation of choice, but presents the antidote. First is the acquisition of wisdom, which brings maturity of mind and heart; then watchfulness in keeping one's steps. But above all (v. 24), have a positive goal ahead of you, and keep your sights on that.

CHAPTER 8

Spoken about in the third person up to this, Wisdom now presents herself in her own voice (v. 4). In this, the most theologically rich chapter in the first book, Wisdom is once again personified, as she was in 1:20; 3:13; 4:6, but the treatment is more fully developed, and her relationship with God and with mankind more intimate. The earlier imagery is maintained, but the use of the imperative is more marked here, and the appeal more personal. Lady Wisdom is the direct opposite of the "loose" or "perverse" woman of the previous chapters: no back alley "at twilight" for her (7:10), but the public highways in broad daylight. Like the sage, she has experienced life and so is in a position to give good advice to the "simple ones". This is her role in chapter 8—teaching youth how to acquire maturity and play a creative role in the world—and to enhance her authority she here presents her credentials.

LADY WISDOM SENDS OUT HER INVITATION. 8:1–11.

8 Does not wisdom call,
does not understanding raise her
voice?

[2]On the heights beside the way,
in the paths she takes her stand;

[3]beside the gates in front of the
town, at the entrance of the
portals she cries aloud:
[4]"To you, O men, I call,
and my cry is to the sons of men.
[5]O simple ones, learn prudence;
O foolish men, pay attention.
[6]Hear, for I will speak noble things,
and from my lips will come what
is right;
[7]for my mouth will utter truth;
wickedness is an abomination to
my lips.
[8]All the words of my mouth are
righteous;
there is nothing twisted or crooked
in them.
[9]They are all straight to him who
understands
and right to those who find
knowledge.
[10]Take my instruction instead of silver,
and knowledge rather than choice
gold;
[11]for wisdom is better than jewels,
and all that you may desire cannot
compare with her.

As is usual with the discourses of Book I, here again the call is for one simple disposition: a willingness to learn, and to acquire wisdom. However classic the invitation may be, the tension is remarkably tightened, for it is Lady Wisdom herself who now intervenes, and proposes the basic requirement—truth and reason (vv. 6–10). It is possible that the plan for the pupil's attention may also serve as a reminder of the first prerequisite—to acquire wisdom demands the personal, intellectual effort on the part of the pupil.

Who is Wisdom? In the general context of Prov 1—9 what is most immediately striking is the similarity between this presentation of the "woman" and the previous ones. Like her predecessor of 1:20, she cries out in a public place. Wisdom calls to all who pass by on the street (v. 4), and therefore her message is not just for one class but is of universal appeal. Unlike the universalism of the prophets, which looked to the future, the universalism of wisdom is for the present time, the now of human existence; and its imperative is not delivered in the atrium of the temple, but in the ambient of secular affairs. Wisdom is competing for attention in precisely that arena where people live their lives, and where they are already preoccupied with affairs. Wisdom's place is thus not the ivory tower, but the arena of daily life, and she wishes to become involved with mankind at every level. Her message is delivered at the crossroads, in the midst of merchants, and shopkeepers and the chattering throng. What she offers to all of them who will listen is discretion and prudence (v. 5), that is, the human quality of mature judgment, the capacity to judge life and cope with it. And she offers this in particular to the "simple ones", unformed youth who are still malleable and capable of learning, or conversely capable of folly if they are not caught in time. To this is added a moral quality, "noble things" in v. 6. Wisdom now becomes more idealistic and indeed more spiritual. Noble things, or natural dignity of life (from the root *ngd*—noble) probably means "courtesy" in its primary sense of nobility of deportment and mind suitable to a court; an interiour quality of "courtliness" and its external manifestation in one's dealings with other people. This is allied to integrity, "what is right", a sense of honour and of goodness. Such a person is described in v. 7 as "true", and in v. 8 as "righteous". In the Old Testament the Hebrew root word *'emet* (rendered as "truth" in v. 7) is a positive attitude towards someone or something, and is determined by one's relationship to that object. It suggests a *code,* a personal set of values or standards by which one lives. "Righteousness" is one's conformity to a divinely established order in the world (see above, p. 100f).

The value of a person so endowed cannot be compared to silver, gold or jewels (vv. 10–11). These are indeed of immense value, but true riches reside in a quality of human life. In keeping with the normal practicality of Proverbs there is no disrespect for material riches and wealth. They are much to be desired, are important in any human scale of values and are necessary to the full life. But what Wisdom offers is more important still. Earthly wealth must exist within the framework of true human values, that which is gained by discipline and knowledge. The interior quality of life that Wisdom presumes to offer is first in importance. Material wealth may enhance this, but its value is ephemeral in comparison. This theme will be taken up once more at the end of the second section which speaks of the fruits of Wisdom in society.

LADY WISDOM AND HER ROLE IN SOCIETY. 8:12–21.

[12] I, wisdom, dwell in prudence,
and I find knowledge and
discretion.
[13] The fear of the LORD is hatred of
evil.
Pride and arrogance and the way of
evil
and perverted speech I hate.
[14] I have counsel and sound wisdom,
I have insight, I have strength.
[15] By me kings reign,
and rulers decree what is just;
[16] by me princes rule,
and nobles govern the earth.
[17] I love those who love me,
and those who seek me diligently
find me.

[18] Riches and honour are with me,
enduring wealth and prosperity.
[19] My fruit is better than gold, even
fine gold,
and my yield than choice silver.
[20] I walk in the way of righteousness,
in the paths of justice,
[21] endowing with wealth those who
love me,
and filling their treasuries.

Wisdom describes herself, first in terms of Old Wisdom and its secular preoccupation—the education of a pupil in "prudence" and "discretion" and all the requisite skills for the attaining of life and goodness; and then in the formula of Later Wisdom—the moral dimension of "fear of the Lord" and the "two ways". What she offers to her hearers is first of all a balanced, ordered society and then she integrates this with a "creation" theology of Yahweh and *his* world. Without her, neither is deemed possible, so she must be taken as seriously as one takes the choice of a life-partner, for she is no less important.

At its most basic level, then, that which wisdom offers here is practical *savoir-faire,* the art of applying prudence and discretion to the affairs of life (v. 12). The paired structure of this pericope is to be noted, for it creates almost a polyphony of matched technical terms that leads to the final prize to be awarded—"righteousness and justice" (v. 20), the true wealth that is sought. In this presentation of Wisdom's role in achieving worldly success (in the best sense of the word) we get a picture of a person who is immersed in worldly affairs—social life, business, administration—no aspect of which is incompatible with wisdom. Indeed, the person so designated leaves the impression of possessing an immense integration of worldly and religious maturity (vv. 12 and 14). In this context, the discipline of wisdom is "fear of the Lord", which is defined as hatred of whatever is evil. It is a question of moral evil, one of the options to be accepted. Thus "fear" in this context is a discipline for life, and an openness not merely to the teacher but to God. It is a return to the concept of "wholeness", but here this is applied equally to secular affairs and to religious life, for all of life is a unity and is ultimately lived before a personal God. This is admittedly a re-interpretation of the older sapiential tradition that lies behind the present redaction of Prov 1—9, but it is the text as it stands that determines the message. So what we have in this chapter is a transition from moral neutrality to commitment. The traditional portrait of the successful statesman or business administrator is now infused with a new quality of "goodness" that envelops the whole of human life, worldly and religious. The concept "life" is seen as the result of a definite choice of the "way". "Perverted speech" (v. 13) anchors it quite firmly in both contexts.

The following verses, 14–16, present all the characteristics of royal, or administrative wisdom. So wisdom takes on a new role; she guides rulers and governments in their appointed tasks. Here also the religious character of "Wisdom" exerts its influence, for "justice" is a divine as well as human quality. In general terms it stands for the truth, and truthful speech and action. In the context of vv. 12–21 it is related to "counsel" (v. 14) which, especially in the later sapiential tradition, stands for God's overall plan for the world of human endeavour (cf. Ps 33 [32]; Job 38:2). Here in 8:14 it reflects the power of Wisdom in human affairs; as an intellectual and religious gift she maintains social order and is responsible for justice. In fact, to the extent that contextually Lady Wisdom identifies with divine characteristics, she can be said to share in the divine nature, a quasi-ontological relationship. The last verses of this section illustrate this point. The vocabulary of vv. 17–21, describing as it does the fruits that flow from docility to the Lady's instruction, is surprising. "I love those who love me", uses the verb *'ahab* for "love", suggesting a note of personal, and very intimate relationship (found also in Sir 4:11–19 and 6:25–31). This form of the verb is quite unusual in sapiential literature, but is found frequently in Hosea and Jeremiah for sensual, and indeed passionate, love. The occurrence of repetitive parallelism in the verse serves as emphasis. The search for Wisdom is almost an act of love, and the resultant relationship is marked by the same intensity. Wisdom "loves" her adherents, and remains totally accessible to them. The use in Hebrew of the independent particle "I", and the repetition of the verbal form in v. 21, reinforce the idea.

What is the effect of this union between Wisdom and the pupil? In the translation the word used is "wealth". In Hebrew it is *yesh,* a state of *being* or of *existence.* The Lady extends to those who love her the qualities of *yesh,* that which has existence, subsists. One lives with her in an atmosphere of "righteousness" and "truth", equity and justice—the ideal of the religious sage, and the fulfillment of the programme set out in 1:3 and 2:9. Wisdom directs one's destiny towards Yahweh, and this search, along with the reciprocity between God and the one who finds him, results in the possession of a treasure most worth having, what may be called the religious conscience. The gifts she bestows include material prosperity, but this is not gross materialism. It is instead part of a whole view of life, of integrated values of the human being as spiritual and material. It results in a comprehensive world-view that sees the human person related to its environment. A dignity that, even when a-religious, is good.

LADY WISDOM AND HER ROLE IN CREATION. 8:22–31.

[22] The LORD created me at the
beginning of his work,
the first of his acts of old.
[23] Ages ago I was set up,
at the first, before the beginning of
the earth.
[24] When there were no depths I was

brought forth,
when there were no springs
abounding with water.
[25] Before the mountains had been
shaped,
before the hills, I was brought
forth;
[26] before he had made the earth with
its fields,
or the first of the dust of the
world.
[27] When he established the heavens, I
was there,
when he drew a circle on the face
of the deep,
[28] when he made firm the skies
above, when he established
the fountains of the deep,
[29] when he assigned to the sea its limit,
so that the waters might not
transgress his command,
when he marked out the foundations
of the earth,
[30] then I was beside him, like a
master workman;
and I was daily his delight,
rejoicing before him always,
[31] rejoicing in his inhabited world
and delighting in the sons of men.

Stylistically, this is almost a new "Creation Narrative", hymnic in form. Another, and more obvious, form of this can be found in Sir 24:3. It reminds one of Gen 1 and Ps 104 (103). Here in Prov 8 Wisdom is said to control human society and to have been present at the creation of the world. These verses constitute a hinge that links the central parts of the chapter, and in some way defines them and illustrates the purpose of the exhortation. Already the reader has been prepared for the ideas found here by v. 13 and v. 17, so the statement takes up a particular point of view, hinted at by the reference to Yahweh (v. 13). Since this belongs to a particular tradition (and we must remember that the Yahweh context is, after all, deliberate) we can understand the whole passage in the light of that tradition. Two questions are dealt with in sequence: the origin of Wisdom, and her function in creation.

The vocabulary, especially of vv. 23–25, is somewhat ambiguous, so it becomes necessary to clarify the words used. Wisdom's claim in v. 22 is that the Lord "created" her. God is the origin of Wisdom, and since this is so the word presumably represents for the author an aspect of the essence of Wisdom, her very nature. But what does it mean? Of itself, the word is unclear—in Hebrew it can mean "create" or "acquire" or even "procreate". The context expands this: v. 23 speaks of her being "set up", but the verbal form used has the connotation of "being hidden". Verse 24 says she was "brought forth", and v. 25 presents her as being "brought forth" or being "born". Each subsequent verb is meant to expand or clarify the first concept of v. 22, so the most probable meaning is "Yahweh created me" or "Yahweh begot me". According to the poetic structure there is thus a threefold stress on the *mode* of Wisdom's coming into being that suggests she was acquired by generation, as God's child. She remains distinct from God, though his own "issue" in some mysterious way. More important from the author's point of view is the question of her priority, and again here there is a poetic, threefold stress. Verse 22 calls her the *"beginning* of his (God's) work, the *first* of his acts". "Beginning" (*re'shît* in Hebrew) is also ambiguous, having both a temporal and a qualitative sense. However, since the supplementary term "first" (*qedem* in Hebrew) has a temporal meaning it is most likely that Wisdom has priority as Yahweh's firstborn in time. She has been begotten by God before the rest of creation, and the following verses carry the same emphasis. As a creation narrative it is singularly different to contemporary foreign wisdom models which tend to stress birth by divine combat or divine intercourse. Prov 8 in comparison has an almost metaphysical austerity. Wisdom's unique relationship to God and her priority in time guarantee the promises she made in vv. 14–21.

Verse 27 brings a slight change in tone, being more placid, more assured, reminiscent both of Gen 1 and Job 38. Here again a problem arises with v. 30—"I was beside him like a master workman". Some texts suggest that the master workman here is God himself, but the grammatical structure—a conjunctive and the absence of the article—supports the idea that it is Wisdom who was the "master workman". Even this word (*'amôn* in Hebrew) is ambiguous, as it can mean a "foreman" (from the Akkadian, a semitic language akin to Hebrew, used in Mesopotamia) or a "favourite child" (from Ugaritic, see above p. 89). If we take it in the first sense there is a sequence from the previous verses, which deal with the divine creative activity, whereas if we take the latter sense there is a natural sequence from vv. 22–24 where Wisdom is God's "firstborn". There is no textual reason for giving either interpretation editorial pre-eminence, so it is possible that the author intended it to be a double concept: Wisdom as firstborn and favoured child of Yahweh, who, craftsman-like, shares his creative activity. This enriched symbolism would accord quite well with the more general context of chapter 8.

Wisdom, though created, is different from the rest of God's creation, the world of human experience. In some way also she is more closely associated with him in his activity. Thus she can be seen as an intermediary, at home with God and man (vv. 30–31). She is at God's side as a collaborator in a creation that most clearly manifests God's wisdom: her objective delight in the presence of God becomes an objective delight in the company of the human race to which she offers herself. There is a great emphasis here on the world and its "created" being. Wisdom, addressing herself to those who will listen, reveals herself as both created and co-creator, and emphasizes the joy in the created world that she can communicate to those who love her. This idea follows easily from her role in society; she orders it well (vv. 12–21) precisely because of her divinely established architectonic role as the "first of the ways of God" (vv. 22–31). Through her, God's act of creation becomes an act of communication: as God goes outside of himself so as to meet mankind on a mutually appreciable level. There he, like Wisdom herself, can "delight in the sons of men."

It is also true that in her role of rapprochement between the divinity and his creation, Wisdom, at once divine and human, stands as a communicator between humanity (the invitation is universal) and the created world, for she reveals to men the key to the ultimate meaning of the universe. Access to God and to the created world is found in a relationship of love with Wisdom (vv. 17 and 21). Wisdom leads us to a comprehension of the design of God. In this way we share a mystery, the very "counsel" of the divinity (v. 14) which transcends all empirical realities, so we are being drawn beyond the ordinary sapiential categories of experience into the very heart of being. Both world and humanity are joyfully encompassed by Wisdom, and tend towards a union with God that is beyond discipline and comes only as a gift.

WISDOM'S FINAL EXHORTATION. 8:32–36.

[32] And now, my sons, listen to me:
happy are those who keep my
ways.
[33] Hear instruction and be wise,
and do not neglect it.
[34] Happy is the man who listens to me,
watching daily at my gates,
waiting beside my doors.
[35] For he who finds me finds life

and obtains favour from the
LORD;
[36] but he who misses me injures himself;
all who hate me love death."

An appeal, in the usual sapiential manner, to the reader to learn from Wisdom herself. The wisdom formula in v. 32—"happy are those"—serves as a final connecting link not only with vv. 1–11 but with all that has gone before in these chapters. The context is still that of the intellectual adventure of "seeking wisdom". A decided note of urgency marks the teacher's final words. The one who would learn is urged, three times in this short section, to "listen": in vv. 32, 33 and 34. The formulation of v. 33 stresses the motive: the *waw* or copula of finality is used, along with the imperative to discipline—"hear instruction, *that you may [thereby] be wise*". Once again we are reminded of the absolute need of discipline if one is to attain wisdom, and wisdom is a matter of life and death, of walking with Yahweh or walking alone. "Who misses me, injures his very being" is a more accurate translation of "himself" (*nepesh*) in v. 36a, and those who "hate me *love* death" in v. 36b returns to the intimate and indeed passionate relationship that previously marked Lady Wisdom's attachment to her followers (vv. 17 and 21).

Wisdom is a rule of conduct, capable of procuring God's special favour for the hearer. Therefore it is dependant on God. With this exhortatory style the chapter closes as it began (v. 4), but here the instruction is expanded and transformed by a new idea (v. 34), emphasized by the use of the wisdom formula. It unifies the whole discourse, for the familiar moralizing tone fits both parts, presenting the gifts that derive from following Wisdom's precepts: in 18–21 life and Yahweh's favour, and here in 35–36. This is reminiscent of the idea found in Ps 1:2 where we find the positive definition of the wise or the good, and it takes up the "courtship" motif found throughout Prov 1—9. The moralizing formulation of the conclusion unifies the whole discourse. Here in vv. 35–36 the profits that accrue from observance of Wisdom's precepts are of the spiritual order, as also were they in vv. 18–21 which they complete: it is a simple choice—life, the favour of Yahweh and a shared joy in creation; or death and oblivion.

What is noteworthy is the fact that Wisdom is presented in a very specific role. It is not a prophetic role, or indeed any documentary or informative role, for the formal "announcement" style is totally lacking. Instead, Wisdom speaks in her own person with her own authority. The intention is to encourage the pupil to cleave to her, to develop a personal relationship with her, so her "attractions" are presented to susceptible youth. It is almost a seductive role that is ascribed to her. She is an acquisition, as the frequent use of "take, receive" in the exhortations makes clear (1:1–5; 4:2; etc.). Her mission is to the created world, and she offers herself there to all who are interested. Along with Sir 24 and Wis 6–8, here we approach the Spirit of God in wisdom present in the world.

CHAPTER 9

Book I closes with an extended proverb or "parable" of two separate invitations to a banquet, thus establishing a diptych form: Lady Wisdom (vv. 1-6) contrasted with Dame Folly (vv. 13–18). The central section is an intrusion, a series of maxims that differ in style from the rest of the chapter. They present a realistic, and traditional view that it is futile to try and educate the incorrigible and the cocksure, so the teacher should concentrate on the docile. This pessimistic view is related to the religious preoccupation, that the basic attitude of the pupil must be "fear of the Lord". This integration of intellectualism and piety is out of context. The parable of antagonism that remains is a fitting conclusion to chapters 1–8, resuming the central theme of two ways, two attitudes to wisdom, and two personifications.

THE BANQUET OF LADY WISDOM. 9:1–6.

9Wisdom has built her house,
she has set up her seven pillars.
[2]She has slaughtered her beasts,
she has mixed her wine,
she has also set her table.
[3]She has sent out her maids to call
from the highest places in the
town,

[4]"'Whoever is simple, let him turn in
here!"
To him who is without sense she
says,
[5]"'Come, eat of my bread
and drink of the wine I have
mixed.
[6]Leave simpleness, and live,
and walk in the way of insight."

A portrait of wisdom, again personified. The reappearance of this lady on the stage expands the concept of the personification of wisdom already seen throughout these chapters by new symbolism, presenting Wisdom as mistress of her "house", inviting the "simple" to share a "meal". The first verse establishes the symbolic value of the imagery. All that follows is to be interpreted as a parable, and is open to be understood and applied in a personal way by each reader. The literal meaning must not be allowed to dominate.

The first illustration, Wisdom's "house", sets the stage. It has seven pillars (the number of "perfection"). A splendid residence to enter is that of Lady Wisdom, an invitation not to be spurned. The meaning may be clarified by reference to chapter 8. This "house" is a symbol of knowledge and learning, the secular and moral discipline that makes one master of the created universe. It is the goal of the sapiential project. And like the wisdom instructor, she invites "the simple", the inexperienced and ingenuous who need to be brought to maturity, and offers them rich food—"bread and wine" and meat. The bread and wine may be cultic, a reminiscence of Gen 14:18 for example, but need not necessarily be interpreted in that way. They can merely represent the staple of life. And it is nourishment for "life" that the Hostess here offers to all those who wish it. Here we have a picturesque re-statement of the formal sapiential invitation, a resumption of 1:20; 8:1. As always, Wisdom's concern is that all may have life in abundance.

In the case of Lady Wisdom, as of Dame Folly later, the invitation is to a banquet, and a rich banquet at that. This is a symbol of life, for it is this that the instruction of the sage traditionally offered. So the personage depicted in 9:1–6 is in fact a personification of the educational process. Wisdom attracts young people, often by the force of her personality, not to worldly enjoyment but to the love of and delight in learning. Leaving behind former companions and a former way of life, the immaturity of character and intellect that marks the "simple", the pupil *gladly* cleaves to the discipline that brings maturity and a personal commitment to knowledge. This is not an action that can be done once and for all, but a process, a path one sets one's feet to and walks along until one reaches the house of wisdom. And that lady uses every seductive process possible, every means at her disposal, to bring about the desired end, the "life" of those she loves, those who are disposed to follow her.

THE BANQUET OF DAME FOLLY. 9:13–18.

[13] A foolish woman is noisy;
she is wanton and knows no shame.
[14] She sits at the door of her house,
she takes a seat on the high places of the town,
[15] calling to those who pass by,
who are going straight on their way,
[16] "Whoever is simple, let him turn in here!"
And to him who is without sense she says,
[17] "Stolen water is sweet,
and bread eaten in secret is pleasant."
[18] But he does not know that the dead are there,

that her guests are in the depths of
Sheol.

Equally drastically, this section presents a portrait of wisdom's antagonist, the personification of foolishness and perversity. Dame Folly is described in v. 13, and her characteristics draw one's mind back to the "strange woman" who shares the stage of Prov 1—9 with Lady Wisdom (cf. 7:11). The reader is introduced to the obverse of the portrait presented so carefully in 8:1—9:6, and the person encountered is an illustrated warning against the temptations one meets with in life, the pitfalls in the path of youth that so naturally preoccupy the teacher and parent. Again the invitation is addressed to the "simple," but the nuance is different, for Dame Folly has a cynicism that looks first to the weakness of youth, so easily turned aside from reaching maturity for the very good reason that no one particularly likes hard work, and discipline is needed if one is to grow in "insight" (cf. v. 6 and Wisdom's invitation). It is not fortuitous that Folly's main characteristic is that she is "noisy" and obtrusive, like a television advertisement. It is characteristic of the "simple" that they tend to listen to the loudest noise and equate loquacity with wisdom. She appeals to the same sort of person—the untutored, the simple, those who prefer to let others think for them; and what she offers is undoubtedly attractive—easy success that the recipient does not realize has been *too* easily gained. Certainly, it is easier to attain than learning.

Wisdom was a "wife", "sister" and "lover" (5:15; 7:4; 8:17); true to the antithetical symbolism of the chapter, Folly is a harlot, a seductress. She has no interest at heart except her own, and from the tone of the text one feels that this is too often tinged with casual amusement. She is not interested in what is lasting, only in death (v. 18), and her appeal is at this level. Her favours are pleasant for a brief spell, but lead to oblivion. She cares nothing for the consequences of her actions, either to herself or to others. Verse

17 provides the key to the parable. The invitation she so casually offers (she does not even leave home to issue it, v. 14) is to a banquet that scarcely exists, and what is positive about it is also perverse. The only attraction it has, in contrast to the rich fare offered by Wisdom, is that it is "stolen" (v. 17) and secret. It has the fatal attraction of dangerous or illegal actions. It offers a fugitive sensation, a moment of intense excitement. The Hebrew text of vv. 14 and 17 conjures up an interesting image. Folly has a very attractive front door, and it is only when one gets inside that one realizes it is in fact the back door to oblivion, and one cannot get out again. Both wisdom and folly cry out in every marketplace, and both proffer "life", but only one lives up to the promise.

Book II
The Proverbs of Solomon
10:1—22:16.

Observations On Life and Behaviour. 10:1—22:16

This is a collection of heterogeneous, and semi-independent, maxims and precepts. In form, they are real "proverbs" in the normally accepted sense of the word, unlike the discourses of Prov 1—9. They are essentially what might be called a "literature of the schools", and resemble a teacher's repertory of educational "sayings" that can be drawn on to impress or inform a group of students. Each one is a single unit, having a particular relevance for each reader, though of course the basic meaning is well worked out and clearly defined. However, personal intuition is still required to draw out the deeper meaning each one has. Though there is little or no connection between them, and no real pattern can be perceived, they all deal with the moral life, a mélange of secular and religious wisdom whose purpose is to help one live an ordered existence in a world that is accepted as being already established according to its own rules.

Almost all are distinguished by the proverbial two-part structure: sometimes analogical—a comparison between two phenomena; but more often antithetic—fool/wise, good/bad, which draws the reader's attention to a given life-situation and its consequences for himself. The imperative style so familiar from Book I is missing here. Instead, the teachers present a certain type of situation that reveals the human consequences that follow a given kind of activity or attitude, and the percipient are enabled to draw a conclusion or evolve a law that may be of practical service to them.

This section of Proverbs is almost entirely secular, the divine or religious dimension being at best secondary, but it does form a kind of horizontal revelation of human activity, at times reflecting the mystery. The authors here have not proposed, and do not intend to propose, two ways of life in dichotomy, as if the human being lived one part of life on a secular plane and another part as a religious person. Both are components, and integral components, of the same entity, and the effects of either the one or the other do not stand in isolation. It is a humanism of a very high order.

Just as in Prov 1—9, we have here a preoccupation with the attaining of "wisdom", but the emphasis differs. Much more in this Book, the object of the wisdom project is the worldly value of life, human life, accessible to all by reasonable effort, yet even here the purely biblical insight remains. The emphasis is secular; life is no longer seen as determined by the sacred, but by the rational and the intellectual. This in fact brings a freshness to morality lacking in the more overtly religious literature. Secularity becomes a particular way of facing reality, a reality that, *naturally and unstrained,* includes the divine. The central sapiential preoccupation is still evident—the desire to perceive the world as susceptible to order, and so to elaborate a series of rules for life that will integrate the individual into the environment: first by understanding the world, then by communicating something of this understanding, and finally by adapting the rules to experience. Like all sapiential teaching, it is based on the most primitive of human drives, the pursuit of life and happiness and success. And the mental flexibility of the sages gives a religious orientation even to the most worldly pursuit. Of course, education still retains its indispensable role in this process.

Though essentially a heterogeneous collection with no central, or key, structural unity, certain sapiential themes surface in the text of 10—22, and while these do not by any means give coherence to the miscellany, they indicate a certain point of view and serve to give something of the "taste" of the proverbial literature.

THE POTENCY OF WORDS. 10:18–21; 31–32.

The whole of this section of Proverbs is marked by the opposition of wise/fool, which almost supplies an editorial key. This antithetic structure dominates the section on "Words", and contrasts the way the fool uses them with the way the wise does.

> [18] He who conceals hatred has lying lips,
> and he who utters slander is a fool.
> [19] When words are many, transgression is not lacking,
> but he who restrains his lips is prudent.
> [20] The tongue of the righteous is choice silver;
> the mind of the wicked is of little worth.
> [21] The lips of the righteous feed many,
> but fools die for lack of sense.
>
> [31] The mouth of the righteous brings forth wisdom,
> but the perverse tongue will be cut off.
> [32] The lips of the righteous know what is acceptable,
> but the mouth of the wicked, what is perverse.

The problem of human language fascinated the sages, as of course they were themselves concerned to make the best possible use of words in communication. This is the only real basis for interpersonal relationships, and words can make or break a community (v. 18 and v. 31). They can bring contentment and harmony (v. 21 and v. 32), and are a source of life. Lying is strongly opposed, it is a deep-seated cancer and has many forms: straight untruth, silly prattling (v. 19), and even the latter is objectionable. Wisdom, morality, religion come together on the subject of words. In v. 18 a favourite idea of the sapiential writers (and of the *tôrôt* of entrance) is put in negative terms—truth in speech is more than a virtue, it is an expression of one's interiority. What one says reflects what one is—communicating, as it were, the colour of one's life. Friendship depends to no small degree on control of, and honesty in, language. It is not necessary always to be in agreement, a good critique can be healthy, but there must be respect for others. There is a certain emphasis on silence, or at least a sparing use of words, for they are a potent force.

Though some of these proverbs may be popular in origin, there is little doubt but that the final nuance of vv. 19–21 has been evolved by a thinker. The central perception is found in the antithesis of "tongue" and "mind"—in Hebrew "heart" (v. 20), and the emphasis is on the dynamic of speech. The speech of a wise person is the fruit of his mind and is creative, whereas the "heart" of the foolish, their inner being and their attitude to life, expressing itself in words can be destructive. Wise here are termed "righteous," so there is a certain moral issue in question. The wise will keep quiet until the time is suitable for talking, and since he weighs his words, what he says will have real influence. A reputation for glibness or talkativeness damages one's reputation. Disciplined speech is an instrument whereby one can handle people and situations. Speech and thought are so related that the words of a sage are food for life *for others* (v. 21), the social dimension is important here, with its material and moral implications (see also 3:14–17).

This whole passage reflects the wisdom point of view, that much talk, of whatever kind, cannot be good: no one can have that much of value to communicate and control is inevitably lost—a cardinal sin in the eyes of the sages (cf. Sir 20:8). The talker is like the drunkard, not only does he injure others, he loses control of his own life. And the sage appeals to the reader's own experience! While the text of vv. 31–32 is not absolutely clear, this small section serves as an *envoi* to the teaching on words and their influence. Again the use of antithesis brings out the meaning (the verbal form in Hebrew is *causative*)—by speaking well, one achieves *life*; by speaking ill, one commits suicide. The term "acceptable" in v. 32 signifies "that which gives pleasure", therefore "falsehood" stands for social strife. Words can penetrate the ego, and strip a person of healthy self-esteem, can morally castrate one. They are very hard to control—once spoken they spread like a bush-fire and their effect is out of all proportion to their size. In themselves words have a timeless, moral value: they are a "fountain of life" (10:11) and a "tree of life" (15:4). They must therefore be handled with care, and be honest, few and well chosen.

RIGHTEOUSNESS AND REMUNERATION. 11:4–11.

This extended proverb is concerned with human and social "righteousness", that is, the human being and its responsibility in the secular sphere. The antithetic structure, common to Prov 10—22, is maintained in these verses.

[4]Riches do not profit in the day of wrath,
but righteousness delivers from
death.
[5]The righteousness of the blameless
keeps his way straight,

but the wicked falls by his own
wickedness.
[6]The righteousness of the upright
delivers them,
but the treacherous are taken
captive by their lust.
[7]When the wicked dies, his hope
perishes,
and the expectation of the godless
comes to naught.
[8]The righteous is delivered from
trouble,
and the wicked gets into it
instead.
[9]With his mouth the godless man
would destroy his neighbour,
but by knowledge the righteous
are delivered.
[10]When it goes well with the righteous,
the city rejoices;
and when the wicked perish there
are shouts of gladness.
[11]By the blessing of the upright a city
is exalted,
but it is overthrown by the mouth
of the wicked.

This takes a fresh look at an old problem. The Old Testament teaching was clear: the righteous are rewarded by God, and the wicked punished. The nature of the remuneration was normally taken to be material prosperity, but these verses add a further nuance by looking at the problem from a secular point of view. The first three verses of this chapter establish the moral principle in terms that derive from Lev 19:26: "a false balance is an abomination to the Lord". This serves as a religious judgement on human conduct, and establishes honesty as the bedrock of social activity. The following verses develop the idea in the secular sphere.

Due to the antithetic parallelism of the passage, the "day of wrath" in v. 4a is clearly death itself (4b), premature and unfulfilled—the final earthly sanction, as in the more religious tradition God is the ultimate sanction. Here in vv. 4–11 the sage has in mind the natural law or ordinary social law (which can be regarded as deriving from God). Material remuneration is in question, but it is not considered the only, or even the best, reward for righteous living. Wealth is not despised—it never is in the wisdom tradition—but it is by no means the most secure refuge, though many wealthy people seem to think of it in this light. What preserves one on the path of life, and makes the way smooth and level (v. 5) is less wealth than certain *human qualities*, uprightness and integrity, which constitute true riches. These establish one's own status, and uphold society. Verse 8 presents the classic thesis of remuneration, and gives it a new twist. The sage is quite well aware of the fact that the righteous are frequently afflicted, but he holds that this is merely temporary, for ultimately they will be rescued, as their path leads in that direction; whereas the wicked is on a road that, whatever be his present state of prosperity, inevitably leads to distress. Recompense in this world is in question, but from the perspective of natural sanctions of life and society. The final verses make this clear, and apply it, v. 10 stating the fact, and v. 11 showing why this is so. The qualities that the righteous person brings to the service of the community—probity, wise counsel—are creative of social good, whereas the wicked are driven by self-interest and greed, have little regard for the rights of others, and destroy society. There is a hint here of retribution by social censure, for such a person, even though wealthy, can not be really respected. A society is clearly built up by the honesty and responsibility of the citizens themselves, who recognize an individual on the basis of his or her contribution. Thus this section shares a common biblical view on the antithesis good/bad, wise/foolish. Prosperity, health, success are determined by fidelity to "right". The orientation is towards people who are good or bad, rather than abstract concepts of "goodness". The reader's attention is turned, not to material prosperity, but to human values such as integrity, justice, righteousness (and their contraries) by the presentation of concrete cases, examples and attitudes rather than by the enunciation of moral principles. This makes morality, and moral teaching, a very vital thing, for it leaves it to the reader to enunciate his own principles of right and wrong on the basis of a set of true standards ("a just balance", v. 1) which he can apply to his own situation. It is not seen as Yahweh imposing a code on the individual, but the individual articulating and evolving a code that best represents his own humanity. Verse 11 sums it up by presenting an illustration of true human wealth: goodness of life that brings stability to a community. Even where material prosperity is absent, there is this quality of life that rewards the upright, renders them stable in themselves and an influence in the community. There remains something ephemeral about the lives of the wicked.

It is clear that this section of Proverbs, as indeed all of Book II, is not interested in "retribution" as such, but in a notion of cause and effect. Righteousness is something dynamic and constructive, evil destructive. Both bring about an effect in society. One who organizes his life properly, according to a positive value, will by that fact be productive in the community of something of value. This is a secular value-pattern, but it is clearly moral, and clearly good. In this context, any reference to God and his influence is important: he takes pleasure, or otherwise, in certain acts (v. 1), he weighs the deeds of men. In these cases where the divine sanction is integrated with the secular, it is meant to raise the latter to a new level without changing its essential secularity. Both these proverbs and the proverbs that make no mention of Yahweh apply a norm to a specific situation; if Yahweh is mentioned it gives the proverb a greater theological directness, but all have in fact an equal theological quality. All refer to a world where God is real. Like all of the Wisdom literature,

Prov 11 approaches the problems of human justice empirically, so the connection between a human act and its social consequences is seen "from outside", as it were. So in fact it is not a doctrine of retribution, for reward (or punishment) is not seen as a forensic act, it derives from the nature of the human action itself. In fact, there is really no word in the Hebrew text of Proverbs for "punishment" in our sense. Two words are used, and both can mean the deed or the consequence. An evil deed initiates a series of consequences that ultimately effect the doer and his community.

GOD AND THE MYSTERY OF EXISTENCE. 16:1–9.

This first section of chapter 16 forms a thematic unit, dominated by the presence of God and the incalculable dimension of human life. The whole chapter is an integration of secular teaching and religious belief: vv. 1–9 being Yahwistic, and 10–15 presenting Royal wisdom. Verses 7–12 serve as a unifying factor, or hinge, linking both types of wisdom. It may be a deliberate editorial effort, but it is more likely to be a natural, spontaneous perception of the complexity of life, which is lived at a level where God is as real as the material dimension is, and the "environment" comprises both. Faith and reason are not opponents, but two sides to one perception of life.

16 The plans of the mind belong to
man,
but the answer of the tongue is
from the LORD.
[2]All the ways of a man are pure in his
own eyes,
but the LORD weighs the spirit.
[3]Commit your work to the LORD,
and your plans will be established.
[4]The LORD has made everything for its
purpose,

even the wicked for the day of
trouble.
[5]Every one who is arrogant is an
abomination to the LORD;
be assured, he will not go
unpunished.
[6]By loyalty and faithfulness iniquity is
atoned for,
and by the fear of the LORD a man
avoids evil.
[7]When a man's ways please the LORD,
he makes even his enemies to be at
peace with him.
[8]Better is a little with righteousness
than great revenues with injustice.
[9]A man's mind plans his way,
but the LORD directs his steps.

The first, Yahwistic, part of chapter 16 is dominated by the presence of God, vv. 1–3 dealing with Yahweh as the directing agency in human life, and vv. 4–7 with Yahweh as director of the moral order. For a parallel treatment of the same principle one can turn to Sir 1:1–10 and Sir 24. This assimilation of wisdom to *Tôrah,* for that is essentially what it is, shows the scribes' preoccupation with the possible theological expansion of the concept of wisdom. The result is an interesting picture of God and the human condition, framed by v. 1 and v. 9. This section insists on God's place in human affairs and human morality. A teaching that is clearly religious is in question. Wisdom procures success in life, and this is seen in terms of the ultimate divine sanction, where the determinative factor is the often unknown divine purpose. God is present in the affairs of humanity (v. 2), and directs the individual to the end he chooses. Even the minor details of this life are of interest to him (v. 7). In v. 1 the antithesis of "heart" ("mind" in the R.S.V.) and the "answer of the tongue"—that is the human project in life and the final outcome of one's thoughts and purposes—is more than a simple contrast of thought and expression. It is a positive statement of God's absolute, and ultimate, control over human affairs and the world of man. In the first place, so much depends on human *judgements,* moral or practical, and to seek to apply these to a world not totally comprehensible to humans is at best inadequate, at worst crass folly (v. 2). Human judgement is of course right and even essential, but it can never be taken as the last word. The perception that "there *are* more things in heaven and earth" than are dreamt of in human philosophy is an essential corollary to life. So v. 1 states a principle that runs through Proverbs: to the human being belongs the task of framing initiatives, of dreaming dreams, but the project must ultimately be expressed effectively in action—and along the way many things may happen which are outside one's control. Not only is God an incalculable, much that is human is so as well: 16:9; 19:14, 21. In his attempts to master life man must remain aware of the limits imposed by humanity. This can be interpreted as comforting or distressing, and often it is both: Qoheleth thinks it comfortable, Job arrives at a compromise, but both see something of the mystery. If we translate v. 1b as "the decision comes from Yahweh" (with Barucq), we think of Yahweh's creative word which is the ultimate answer, and determines the shape of events. Human plans will succeed only if they coincide with the divine plan.

Here stands the fundamental antithesis of man and God. God and his divine administration remains a mystery, God alone directs the world on its way according to his own rules. And while the human intellect is free to question or to research the ultimate "why?" of things the answer remains too often hidden with God. This idea is resumed in v. 9, where we see that a man's intentions and activity only have validity within the context of the divine providence. He must plan and act, that is his human vocation, but he must be totally disposed to whatever end God intends. It is, in its way, an integration of reason and faith. Genius comes from God; the talented person can work and produce, but the ultimate end is the domain of genius. Here Proverbs deals, as later it will do in 20;24, not with experience, but with the unknown. One cannot fully trust one's own perception, for what one thinks of value can appear different in the divine perspective. Never approach life with too much confidence in your ability to understand. Indeed, v. 3 re-establishes confidence in the project of the human mind. It might well be translated—"direct your work towards the Lord", in which case it suggests that the human project, limited though it be, accords with the divine plan, because it accords with the human propensity to search for the "reason why". So even if the result is not what one could hope for, if one meets failure rather than success, on the real level it is all successful because it is the dynamic thrust that is vital, man is born to dream and to strive; in that he proves himself truly human.

The divine government of the world remains the only absolute, and there is a purpose behind it all, a reason for the way things are. There might be here a suggestion of an answer to the problem of theodicy, a concept of act-consequence inherent in the scheme of things. Verse 4 notes that everything is made "for its purpose", even the wicked. Even the inexplicable has a function.

Verse 5 takes up a new idea, and even the style changes to accommodate it. The formula "abomination to the Lord" recalls the Yahwistic tradition, and introduces the concept of moral retribution, giving it a new twist for the sapiential literature. Sooner or later, things will be seen to balance out. Verse 6 takes up the refrain, and presents a theologically central idea (reminiscent in its way of Hos 6:6). "Atoned for" is an example of priestly vocabulary, conjuring up the act of atonement by ritual sacrifice. The idea undergoes theological metamorphosis in the hands of the sages. Here atonement is made, not by cultic act or ritual, but by "loyalty and faithfulness", total internal and external assent to the will of Yahweh. The parallel structure of the verse is important. Verse 6b is a deliberate counterpart of v. 6a, so "fear of the Lord" stands in parallel to the classic religious virtues of loyalty and faithfulness. Where fear of God exists evil is avoided and one lives free from sin. Life is viewed in the usual sapiential terms as a journey; for the just the path is level and free of obstacles and one can live in comfort and reach one's goal. Ethical integrity turns aside the effects of sin on one's way, and relationship with God is maintained. This is a wisdom re-interpretation of the *Tôrah* concept of sacrifice for sin, and instead of ritual it places emphasis on the human dispositions of mind and conduct. It forms a synthesis of human life, and as such underlines the social effects of good or evil conduct. The one whose manner of life is pleasing to Yahweh radiates peace and reconciliation in his society. Because he is righteous God is with him in his endeavours, and this relationship enables him to incorporate even his enemies into the sphere of his own peace; he becomes a remedy for alienation within his own community.

Different though these two parts may be, the one theme runs right through the chapter, turning up in vv. 1, 9, 25 and 33. It may not dominate, but it is present. Irrespective of man's powers of judgement or plans for life God is the ultimate arbiter, and unless he implements it nothing is achieved by human effort. Verses 1, 2 and 9 explore the basic antithesis of God and man, and rouse in the reader an awareness that limits must be set to empirical wisdom, and at this boundary man must submit.

Verse 1 and v. 9 form an inclusion, and it is probable that the sages intended this to be a frame for their particular appreciation of life, in terms of an antithesis between man and God, the comprehended and the unknown. It is man's part to use his mind, to think about life as he knows it, to make plans; but this is never enough *to effect* what he wishes. He must articulate the thought, for what is decisive is to give expression to the human project, and in between thought and effect there lies a whole process that can go wrong at any time (v. 9). While in most proverbs the fundamental duality—between man, the secular and God, the divine—is dealt with on parallel levels, there are some theologically daring proverbs that deliberately present the divine/human antithesis without presenting any answers. Such is 16:1–9—an awareness of human events and perception in tandem with an awareness of God's presence and influence, and the God-dimension parts company with the human. This has a pedagogic function. There are occasions on which the teachers deliberately take the pupil away from the certainty of personal experience and perception, and make him face the fact that there are things beyond human knowing (another example is 20:24). They aimed at tossing their pupils right into life with its variety of perceptions, in the sphere of different and even contradictory experiences of life. Thus, faced both with knowledge and mystery the pupil could get involved in the adventure of life *at first hand,* and even contribute to the process of intellectual co-ordination. They were encouraged to experience life, use their intelligence to the full, and then realize that there yet remained a dimension beyond control and beyond reason.

THE PRINCIPLES OF GOOD GOVERNMENT. 16:10–15.

[10] Inspired decisions are on the lips of a
king;
his mouth does not sin in judgment.
[11] A just balance and scales are the
LORD'S;
all the weights in the bag are his
work.
[12] It is an abomination to kings to do
evil,
for the throne is established by
righteousness.
[13] Righteous lips are the delight of a
king,
and he loves him who speaks what
is right.

[14] A king's wrath is a messenger of
death,
and a wise man will appease it.
[15] In the light of a king's face there is
life,
and his favour is like the clouds
that bring the spring rain.

This section offers a complete change in style, presenting court morality rather than religious, royal wisdom rather than yahwistic. It presents the ideal of good government, which has the function of establishing justice among people. Verse 10 speaks of "inspired decisions" on the lips of a king. The idea is not that God speaks through the king, for the section is consciously secular, but the more sapiential idea that the gift of good government comes from human nature and is a quality of human life. Naturally this is ultimately a creational gift of God, but this dimension plays no real role here. The ideal ruler, acting as a mature and wise human being, will (it is hoped) automatically form judgements that are in accordance with order and justice. The idea is not dissimilar to the concept of wisdom's influence on the ruler in 8:14–16. The universalist note here is predominant; the section applies to all government, and not just to Israel, and the divergence from the religious attitude of the prophets is marked. For them, the king rules by the help of God, and divine guidance is central. In Prov 16 the king rules by intelligence and reason, and by a human perception of justice.

In v. 11 it might be more in keeping with the context to read that "a just balance and scales are the king's", for this is clearly royal wisdom, and so the use of the word "Lord" is an intrusion, possibly from vv. 1–7. The ruler is supreme arbiter of peace and justice, and his role in society is analogous to that of Yahweh in the universe, but in fact Yahweh is not seen in the Old Testament as an arbiter of commercial and social justice. Verse 12 also uses an interesting term in this same context: "an abomination", (*to'eba*) is reminiscent of Leviticus, and suggests that the ruler should be a model of justice because even secular justice reflects the cosmic plan of God. Indeed, for v. 12 justice is not only what is right, it is what is expedient to a ruler. Human wisdom sees that only a just government can hope to enjoy any degree of permanence. And on a practical level this means that the ruler must look to the integrity of his associates and counsellors as well as to his own probity. It is a very human world, and the sage had a cool and realistic view of human government. An idealist is only viable as a ruler if he has equally honest associates (v. 13).

Proverbs exalts the institution of government, and possibly this is a residual influence of its origins in the royal court. The first thing the reader notices is that here the "king" is an ideal, a universally applicable abstraction, suitable for all countries and all forms of government. There is no mention of the Davidic dynasty or of local characteristics, so the portrait remains on the international plane throughout. While royalty is indeed the type of government spoken about, it seems that Prov 16 knew of no other form of rule. True to their tradition, they spoke from their experience. Wisdom confers authority on government, and forms the basis of its fundamental character and role—*justice.* The primary purpose of a government is to ensure to its citizens the rule of justice (16:10; 20:8; 31:5), and to care for the individual, especially the ones most in need (29:14; 31:8–9). This is the ultimate guarantee of stability (16:12; 20:28; 25:5). Any form of oppression is an injustice, and its fruit is anarchy. Verse 14 shows how watchfulness on the part of the ruler is what keeps the peace, but there can arise situations in which sanctions become necessary—it is dangerous to stir up any human government. Perhaps vv. 14–15 reflect a certain sly humour? Advice should be taken from carefully selected advisers, especially if the decision to be made is crucial, and a little humility might on occasion be salutary—after all, only God is all-knowing.

In these two sections of Prov 16 we have religious experience (of Yahweh and his order) alternating with experience of the world (the social order). This reflects the world of Proverbs, a world in which there was little perceptible tension between secular and religious, and human existence was seen as a whole.

THE PRINCIPLES OF A JUST SOCIETY. 22:1-4.

22 A good name is to be chosen
rather than great riches,
and favour is better than silver or
gold.
[2]The rich and the poor meet together;
the LORD is the maker of them all.
[3]A prudent man sees danger and
hides himself;
but the simple go on, and suffer
for it.
[4]The reward for humility and fear of
the LORD
is riches and honour and life.

The basic principle is established in v. 1 with an idea that is unique to Proverbs: the conjunction of "good name" and "favour" is unusual in the text of the Old Testament. Its presence here is possibly due to the prevailing concept in the book of the interior dimension of act and intention. A good reputation, because it is the external expression of the high moral and intellectual quality of the holder, is of more value in establishing a just society than any social or political policy could ever be. It will build up the community *from within.* This is a wisdom insight, that one individual *can* do something about the world if possessed of the right qualities. This is the goal of wisdom. And typical of the sapiential tradition, there is a recognition of reality. In v. 2 we see how rich and poor live together in every society. Equality is thus an ambiguous term—people are scarcely equal, for there are very apparent social differences even in a "perfect" society, and inequalities of gifts and of condition. Only in one thing does equality exist—all have been created by Yahweh, so all have *created* rights and obligations, and this is the only rational basis for the concept of equality in the community. The only "rights" one has are those that pertain to the *human* state, that derive from the divine creative act. The lowest common denominator is the mutual recognition of shared humanness. Indeed, v. 3 begins to distinguish the various social types. The "prudent one" is the one who is sagacious and observant—human qualities both; one who can judge a situation, see any possible source of danger or injury, and take steps commensurate with the danger. He is neither cowardly, nor cold-blooded—that is not the meaning of *'arûm* (prudent) in Hebrew, but a person with foresight and perceptiveness. Human qualities of discretion are indispensable in society.

The final verse introduces the religious and moral element with the formula "fear of the Lord", presented here in unusual circumstances. "Humility" here is deceptive. It is not to be taken as one's recognition of lowliness—irrelevant here—but as a synonym of "fear of the Lord" in its practical application to life in community. Being strange, the combination forces the reader to think again. A just society is founded on a realistic recognition of each one's created nature, and the basic rights and obligations that belong to this state, for others as well as for oneself. The foundation stone of human justice is the fact that it represents the horizontal dimension of the divine "love". It is a recognition of a natural, that is a created relationship, and has nothing to do with equality in the sense of measure or degree.

The reward for this socially constructive attitude is "riches, and honour and life" (v. 4b), that is, both material and spiritual well-being. The sages readily recognized the advantages of material comfort and material wealth. It made for stability and for human expression. A poor person is in some sense enslaved (22:7), but this can be humanly offset by the possession of wisdom, reputation or dignity (22:1). Dependant on the character of the subject, poverty can at times be better than riches; it may lead to tranquillity, whereas riches may lead to dissolution. The real basis on which social justice rests is not a class-levelling, but an attitude to others that reflects the created dignity each has as a human being, and the common relationship with the Creator. He has placed both poor and rich in their situation of life, both can be seen as gifts. Life itself is the great gift, and the use one makes of this is the real treasure to be sought after. Social justice is, therefore, something that results from a cool and rational assessment of what is due to someone on the basis of created nature; it is the communitarian application of that right relationship that is due to the status of human being. However, the material dimension is also important. Proverbs clearly envisages a society in which there is room for everyone to attain a decent level of subsistence, if not riches, a society in which intelligence and hard work can bring anyone, however lowly, to affluence, or at least comfort. That such a society did not exist at the time was quite well-known to the sages, but the principle of human effort and its due level of material achievement is so central to their teaching that the reader must look behind the text itself to perceive the ideal of society that was hoped for, or at least advocated.

Book III
The Words of the Wise
22:17—24:22

Collected Instructions of a Teacher. 22:17—24:22.

This collection, entitled "words of the wise" by the author, is marked out as a unit by the fact that the title of the section beginning with 24:23—"These also are sayings of the wise", is a repetition of 22:17—"hear the words of the wise". This is mistakenly included in the section as its first verse, but in fact it should be taken as the title of the three chapters. It has all the appearances of a teacher's text book, and is most probably adapted from the Egyptian *Instruction of Amen-em-ope*. Like that, it has thirty "sayings" (22:20), loosely brought together. Of these, at least ten closely resemble the Egyptian text. It can be subdivided into two sections: 22:17—23:14, consisting of an introduction (vv. 17–21) and warnings; and 23:15—24:22, counsels, prohibitions and an appeal to the moral sense of the reader. The style is different to that of the previous section, being a direct, and even affective address to the reader, in which argumentation and description predominate, and the intimate teacher-pupil relationship is recalled.

INJUNCTION TO APPLY ONESELF TO LEARNING. 22:17–21.

[17] Incline your ear, and hear the words
of the wise,

and apply your mind to my
knowledge;
[18] for it will be pleasant if you keep
them within you,
if all of them are ready on your
lips.
[19] That your trust may be in the LORD,
I have made them known to you
today, even to you.
[20] Have I not written for you thirty
sayings
of admonition and knowledge,
[21] to show you what is right and true,
that you may give a true answer to
those who sent you?

These verses introduce the collection in traditional wisdom style—it is a teacher's injunction to docility and assiduity. If the reader wishes to be a success in life (v. 18), then he must apply himself to the task of learning, and the first step is attention to those who are already learned. But it does not stop there, so it is essential that the reader be well-motivated, and the teacher goes on to mention the motives that drive the student of wisdom: the expectation of success and worldly prosperity; a maturing of one's religious commitment (v. 19); the need of wisdom if one is to become good at one's task—administration, the public services, or whatever it be as a citizen (v. 21). Verse 19, giving the religious motivation, seems to be an intrusion, and may indeed represent a later editor's effort at integrating religion and the secular. It inculcates a healthy religious attitude of "trust", which in Hebrew has a particular significance. In the wisdom tradition "trust", from the root *batah,* almost completely replaces the more common "faith" (*'mn*). Changed times called for a changed concept of faith, and of the God-man relationship conjured up by the word. It is possibly this preoccupation that is represented by Prov 22:19. In an age when wisdom had replaced law, and the preoccupation was centered on the individual, "trust" seemed a more viable attitude than "faith". It is a more subjective attitude, the result of one's own learning and study, a trust based on personal experience (cf. 3:5). The wise one knows he is in God's hands, so his confidence is not geared to a *future* reality, but is an actual attitude to the God who disposes of human existence.

This new introduction to the concept of study and learning is realistic. Instruction results in wisdom only to the extent that one uses it as the raw material for a personal creative effort, and that a personal synthesis results (v. 21). It is then that wisdom becomes a way of life. One must be able to perceive truth for oneself. The tone of these verses presupposes a community in which learning is prized, and the work of the scholar respected. Study and effort are seen as the only reliable door to human success, that is, the acquisition of learning and of religious commitment. This collection of "words" takes up again the wisdom project.

FAMILY LIFE. 23:22–25.

[22] Hearken to your father who begot
you,
and do not despise your mother
when she is old.
[23] Buy truth, and do not sell it;
buy wisdom, instruction, and
understanding.
[24] The father of the righteous will
greatly rejoice;
he who begets a wise son will be
glad in him.
[25] Let your father and mother be glad,
let her who bore you rejoice.

This paragraph interrupts the sequence of short instructions that makes up chapter 23. It may have been added here by an editor, but in fact it would probably fit in more smoothly after 22:21.

Stylistically, these verses could be taken as the personalized wisdom instruction of a teacher, and indeed it has many of the characteristics of the genre. However, the double mention of "father" and "mother", almost forming an inclusion in v. 22 and v. 25, along with the intimate tone of the injunctions in vv. 22b, 24b and 25, suggests that the instruction in question pertains to the home, which is the first ambient of education, and that it depicts the climate of the ideal home. Wisdom is passed on by those who have acquired it, elders or parents, to a youth with whom they are personally involved and who is amenable to listening to, and accepting, their discipline. In turn, the parents' consolation is a child who grows in both "wisdom" and "justice", and so fulfills all their expectations. On closer analysis, these verses really have little to do with *education* as such, but deal with the home situation, the relationship that should exist between parents and children, a relationship of honour and responsibility. It tells the reader little about the content of the instruction, and quite a lot about attitudes.

Family and social life rank high among the sage's preoccupations, for it is quite bluntly the bedrock of order and stability for any community. Naturally—at least from the teacher's point of view if not from the pupil's—experience is a determinative factor, though it is not exclusive, for not only is the parent not necessarily right all the time, there is also the factor of religious inspiration which has its own role to play—the gift of wisdom follows the gift of life. This is a reminder that for Proverbs morals are frequently a family affair. It is all too easy for a parent to see only one side of the coin, and for this reason vv. 22–25 is careful to present both sides. Respect for parents is the child's part in all this, a respect that endures even when the parent is clearly losing control of bodily and mental faculties (v. 22) and is no longer "respectable". On the broader level wisdom is impossible without a preliminary docility, and for this reason one is seldom quite sure, in the instruction genre, whether parent or teacher speaks. The emphasis in these verses make it probable that family respect is in question, and its first manifestation is openness to parental instruction and a personal regard for elders. At this level, education is an act of love, given and received, and an openness to love. A well-educated, and well-conducted child is a primary source of family stability. Here the educational task is seen as a shared project in which each parent plays a role. This idea is marked in Proverbs (1:8; 4:3; 6:20; 31:1, 26). And it is worth noting that even at this level humour is not wanting (23:13–14): "Do not withhold discipline from a child; if you beat him with a rod, he will not die!" The point here is that human nature is somewhat perverse, and good habits, which are the foundation stones of education, do not generally come too easily, but have to be cultivated.

On the child's part the first requirement is reverence, and a willingness to listen to the ideas garnered by the old —it is thus one inserts oneself into one's tradition and takes hold of one's roots in a community. For this reason continuity between the generations is essential to both old and young. A generation-gap is seldom due to a one-sided inadequacy.

THE DRUNKARD'S LAMENT. 23:29–35.

[29] Who is woebegone?, who is
sorry for himself?,
who is sick, and complaining?;
who has wounds he cannot explain?,
whose eyes are bloodshot?
[30] The one who has lingered
over wine
and has taken to trying
mixed drinks!
[31] Do not linger over the wine,
red and sparkling

in the cup;
indeed, it goes down so smoothly.
[32] But afterwards it is like
snakebite,
like the poison of a viper.
[33] Your eyes see strange things,
and mind and speech lose
co-ordination.
[34] You are left like one
who is prostrate at sea,
who sways like the top
of the mast.
[35] Saying, "someone struck me,
but I did not feel it,
I was beaten, but I did
not know it."
When shall I wake up?, for I
shall need another drink.

(*translation by the author*)

This is a little gem, one of the finest pieces of imaginative writing in the whole of the Book of Proverbs, and though one may find a moral in it—and vv. 31–32 is straight moralizing—it would be a mistake to take it as serious instruction, since it is meant to raise a laugh, and perhaps a wry memory!

The first verse begins, unusually for the context, not with an exhortation (as 22:17; 23:22, 26) but with a series of interjections that underline the dramatic quality of the vignette. One already feels one's temples throbbing: "O woe!, O sorrow!, O strife!" This is of course a warning, and 29b is undoubtedly the sage's summary of the folly of this sort of indulgence, but humour predominates. Technically, the text presents a sketch that illustrates the vice of drunkenness, depicting both the psychological and the physical effects. Clearly, the subject belongs to the same category as the fool, the sluggard and the adolescent; that is, one who loses control and hurts no-one but himself. It can stand as a practical example of the law of act-consequence. It depicts an individual for whom the whole of the wisdom project has been a failure: "without cause" he has wounded himself (v. 29b). Either as a form of escapism, a flight to a false "*shalôm*" far from the hard realities of life; or out of weakness and a loss of self-control, a cardinal vice.

Really, however, it should not be taken too technically. The author is clearly enjoying himself, and means the reader to do so as well. Verse 29 gives a description of the drunkard as he appears to those who meet him next morning. Taken in conjunction with v. 32 and v. 34 it marks the whole passage as being a piece of humour, pure and simple. A moral it certainly contains, but this should not be laboured, for it scarcely has anything to do with the real fun of the scene, the irresistible humour of the passage is probably the primary reason for its insertion here. It describes a hangover: that feeling of having been bitten by a snake; that difficulty in focusing mind or eyes (v. 33); a tendency to jump at sharp noises (which are magnified in your mind); that uneasy speculation as to how on earth the evening ended (v. 35ab), as one feels the bruises. Verse 34 is a classic, giving a picture of the staggering gait of the drunkard, rolling like the mast of a small boat on the high seas, with the horizon surging up and down in a most unnatural way and the ground very unsteady. And the final touch in v. 35: for experience has taught him how painful the effects are, but once recovered he is not going to let that cramp his style. He overdid it, and well he knows it; but when the hangover is gone, perhaps a few more drinks will go down well?

THE SOCIAL VALUE OF WISDOM. 24:3–7.

[3]By wisdom a house is built,
and by understanding it is
established;
[4]by knowledge the rooms are filled

with all precious and pleasant
riches.
[5]A wise man is mightier than a strong
man,
and a man of knowledge than he
who has strength;
[6]for by wise guidance you can wage
your war,
and in abundance of counsellors
there is victory.
[7]Wisdom is too high for a fool;
in the gate he does not open his
mouth.

A short treatise on the value of wisdom, in two steps. Verses 3–4 show its utility in the home, and vv. 5–6 show its value in war. It is purely secular wisdom that is now in question.

The first two verses form a quatrain that presents the architectonic character of wisdom, which builds a house and then furnishes it with all that is needful and good. Three terms are used: wisdom, understanding, and knowledge, and these are synonymous. As in 1:2–6, the effect is meant to be cumulative. Wisdom is here far too rich a concept adequately to be defined by any one term. It is a many-faceted quality of the human person, and so three concepts are joined to communicate its value. It is immediately noticeable that here we are dealing with purely secular wisdom. All three words express practical sagacity, with no moral or religious overtones. What we have here is human knowledge and human ability. The "house" in question (v. 3) is not as such a metaphor, but signifies the actual edifice, walls and rooms; but it can also, by extension, stand for family life, the prosperity and stability of which depends on the day to day exercise of human wisdom.

In the next verses (5–7) we have a clear antithesis between intellectual ability and physical strength, in the context of war and security. This is a favourite theme with international wisdom—all one need do is recall the engaging advice of the teacher from the New Kingdom period of Egypt. This period occurs from about 1570–1300 B.C., and was a time of intellectual renewal, naturalism in art, and a concern for cultural renewal. A teacher's advice from this period reads: "do not be a soldier"; instead, the pupil is advised to follow the scribal vocation and "put writing in your heart". It is ultimately more effective in affairs. In this section of Prov 24 we have Royal Wisdom, effectively if not formally. The setting is that of the court counsellor, often in the sapiential tradition a synonym for the sage. By sage counsel, both security and leadership are ensured to the community, in civil as well as political arenas. There is more in question here than mere practical statecraft or generalship. Wisdom itself, as a human quality of mind, is seen to be the bedrock of social life. In v. 7 the text closes with a contrast to wisdom, by reintroducing the figure of "the fool". He can make no use of wisdom and its treasury. What is unusual here is the fact that, contrary to his usual characteristic in Proverbs (see for example 17:28; 18:6; 29:11), he exhibits his folly by his refusal or inability to "open his mouth". The context is clearly determined by v. 7b. "In the gate" carries with it the suggestion of the public assembly of elders, traditionally held at the gate of the city (see Job 29:7–25). So the folly of the person depicted here has a social context: it would seem to be his inability to serve the common weal by sage advice, or possibly his refusal to face his public duty in giving testimony in a court of law. This points the teaching of the section: wisdom is essentially a *humanizing* element in society, supplying material needs, and standing for the human values of peace, justice and security.

RESPONSIBILITY AND HUMAN RIGHTS. 24:10–12.

[10] If you faint in the day of adversity,
your strength is small.
[11] Rescue those who are being taken

away to death;
hold back those who are stumbling
to the slaughter.
[12] If you say, "Behold, we did not
know this,"
does not he who weighs the heart
perceive it?
Does not he who keeps watch over
your soul know it,
and will he not requite man
according to his work?

The text of v. 10 is somewhat corrupt, but it is still possible to establish the general meaning, and it introduces another wisdom preoccupation, one's duty to society, and to human beings who must be allowed to retain their rights, even when they have transgressed a law of society. While the opportunity exists, one must be ready to grasp it. Those who are being "taken away to death", in v. 11a, are presumably those who have been condemned to death by either the civil or the military authorities. Verse 11b, "stumbling to the slaughter", is synonymous parallelism with v. 11a. We are dealing therefore with the duty to ransom prisoners of war, and the parallel duty to aid those legally accused and condemned—each as the situation requires. And the only rights that remain to these categories of people are human rights. The vigour and emphasis of the language in these verses make it quite clear that here again it is a question of secular wisdom; so the rescue is seen as a natural, and not a "moral" rescue of "sinners whose path leads down to death", as in Prov 14:12 and 16:25, for example. It is not a matter of spiritual aid; what is in question is the plight of the prisoner and the condemned who may be deprived of the rights that remain to him as a human being, even if he has offended against a recognized law. And v. 12 makes it clear that it is not sufficient to plead ignorance, for one has a duty to know what is going on in one's society. Nor can one claim to be uninvolved. One must be aware of one's duty in conscience, and it is here that the sages saw the function of "wisdom"—it is the protector of the conscience. Of course, it may quite validly be the case that one is unable to help—but remember that God will ultimately judge whether this is true or not (v. 12b). "He who weighs the heart" shows the influence of Egyptian wisdom, where Anubis, the god of death, weighs the suppliant's heart on the balance of *ma'at,* or truth.

The central insight of this pericope is that even the condemned have rights. Add to this the fact that the law is at best an imperfect defender of justice, and can err, and one sees that it is a duty of every educated and perceptive individual to try and protect the rights of the condemned. Basically, this is a warning against indifference, against an attitude of "it is none of my business"—and feigned ignorance is no excuse. In the society the sages sought to build no-one can afford the luxury of standing on the sidelines and saying "I am not involved, it has nothing to do with me." One may not avoid one's duty to preserve human values and human rights.

THE NECESSITY OF RESTRAINT. 24:15–20.

[15] Lie not in wait as a wicked man
against the dwelling of the
righteous;
do not violence to his home;
[16] for a righteous man falls seven
times, and rises again;
but the wicked are overthrown by
calamity.
[17] Do not rejoice when your enemy falls,
and let not your heart be glad
when he stumbles;
[18] lest the LORD see it, and be
displeased,
and turn away his anger from him.

[19] Fret not yourself because of
evildoers,
and be not envious of the wicked;
[20] for the evil man has no future;
the lamp of the wicked will be put
out.

The "Instruction" genre is somewhat more obvious in this section than it was in the previous verses, and to some extent this fact leaves its mark on the teaching of the passage. The context changes from the "fool" (v. 7) to a more pernicious type, the "wicked". The wise pupil will not turn to despise the evil person, he will avoid *any* contact with him, or any relationship to him, even that of sanction. It is far better to leave such to their own devices and their own inevitable end—after all, touch dirt and you will become dirty. The whole passage represents the insertion of a religious motivation into the social and secular view of community life proper to this section of Proverbs. Vengeance, or even recrimination, is out of place for the human agent.

The atmosphere evoked by the opening verses, 15–16, suggests that the author had in mind an era of actual violence and injustice, and meant to deal with a real situation, and not just an abstraction conveniently called "unstable government". The ambient seems to be urban. The author underlines the point by adding a positive principle (in v. 16)—that either secret or open violence leads only to failure, and that nothing really constructive can be achieved by those who use destructive weapons as a means to an end (v. 16). It is far more difficult to *re*-create what one has destroyed than to improve what exists. While the initial idea is that of personal integrity which, once destroyed, can scarcely be re-constituted, the final idea is more likely that of divine retribution. This is borne out by the antithetic structure of vv. 15–16, and the use of the terms "wicked" and "righteous", which in the Hebrew Old Testament are *moral* concepts. The terms "rejoice" and "be glad", in v. 17, normally signify for the Hebrew text an outward and perceptible manifestation of exulting, an external expression of joy, malicious or generous. To this v. 18 adds the positive religious aspect: it is not a question that God will be moved one way or another by one's malicious pleasure in the certain punishment of the wicked, for the emphasis is not on the negative "turning of God's anger from him", but the implication that he will turn it *on you.* The proverb is addressed to *the reader,* not to a putative opponent.

In this, the one who has had the opportunity to acquire wisdom is the greater offender. He should have thereby appropriated "fear" as Proverbs sees it, a moral conscience that should be able to replace a direct application to Yahweh's displeasure (v. 18), something that is proper to the morality of the book. The moral, and here religious, principle, is underlined: one may never rejoice at the misfortune, or the wickedness, of others—and as is usual with the proverb style this implies a positive attitude rather than a negative on the part of the reader: what, then, should be *your* attitude to the moral outsider? Certainly, it is not possible to take vengeance; but it is not possible either to simply "leave vengeance to the Lord"; the sages go further. Moderate any desire for vengeance at all on your part; seek the interior quality of detachment (24:17–18). A change of heart is what can most influence your environment. One who harbours vengeance, even for the putative "sake of the Lord", or who takes joy in the misfortune even of an enemy, is himself sick, and thus is himself not so very different from the "wicked". For it is an abiding thought that God not only punishes the wicked —he forgives them (24:15–20). All in all, what inspires the scribe is a noble desire for equity (see also Sir 28:1–7).

Objectively, the wicked have already established their due end, and one would be foolish to vitiate one's own *shalôm* or one's own humanity by a shallow act of vengeance or personal spite (vv. 19–20). The phrase used in these verses is a remarkably strong one for Proverbs (used elsewhere only in 23:18), and indeed for the sapiential tradition, and the repetition here in the text of Prov 24 serves as an emphatic: the wicked one "has no future", his "lamp is extinguished". His existence can no longer be considered a *life*, for it is empty of real meaning. This is a re-statement of the sapiential thesis of act and consequence. The whole of this insight, presented by vv. 15–20, brings us back to the perception of Ps 1, that wisdom statement *par excellence*. Quite naturally, without any human intervention or human sanction, the end of the wicked is dissolution—"chaff blown away by the wind" (Ps 1:4). So Prov 24:20 is not a condemnation of the wicked—if it were, the just would be told how to react positively, and in the text they are not—but it is a warning to the wise of the *inherent* value of a particular wisdom perspective for life.

An Appendix To The Words Of The Wise. *24:23–34.*

This is quite a short section, distinguished from what went before by a title: "these also are sayings of the wise" (v. 23a). It is an appendix to the "words of the wise" in 22:17—24:22, probably added by the editor himself, since v. 23a is a reference back to 22:17, and the tone remains consistent. It first presents a legal maxim, in 23b–29, and then a pen-portrait of the "sluggard", in 30–34. In its own way, it maintains the antithesis of wise/fool, central to this part of Proverbs.

THE PRACTICALITIES OF JUSTICE. 24:23–29.

[23] These also are sayings of the wise.

Partiality in judging is not good.
[24] He who says to the wicked, "You
are innocent,"
will be cursed by peoples,

abhorred by nations;
[25] but those who rebuke the wicked
will have delight,
and a good blessing will be upon
them.
[26] He who gives a right answer
kisses the lips.
[27] Prepare your work outside,
get everything ready for you in the
field;
and after that build your house.
[28] Be not a witness against your
neighbour without cause,
and do not deceive with your lips.
[29] Do not say, "I will do to him as he
has done to me;
I will pay the man back for what
he has done."

Justice, honest speech, home life and a shunning of personal vengeance, these are the keystones to social life as presented by this short section. It begins with a legal maxim, v. 23b, which is then expanded and commented on. A clear contrast is drawn between the unjust, partisan judge who sells his judgement for favour or friendship, and the upright, honest one. Again the theme of "words" is introduced, and their social influence. No one, and much less someone with a community responsibility, can afford to be a respecter of persons or make false statements. The judge, the lawyer, the policeman must be *seen* to give honest testimony.

Another important factor in social life is the family, v. 27, the keystone of community stability. Therefore, it is imperative that people think long and carefully before assuming the married state. The founding of a family is probably in question here, and it is a warning that one must be sure of one's ability to support a family, one must look to one's natural resources, before entering on domesticity. This is an important injunction in the context, for a family of one's own was the natural expectation of every Israelite.

Leaving family matters, vv. 28–29 returns to the court of law, and the scene of forensic justice. There is a suggestion here in the first verse that malice is a canker in society that will ultimately destroy it. It is probably an admonition against too freely entering into litigation, or volunteering your services against a defendant out of motives of revenge. Certainly this is the case in the last verse of this section. It suggests that the best idea of all is to keep clear of lawsuits if humanly possible. Here again we have a sapiential re-interpretation of the *Tôrah* which modifies the traditional Old Testament concept of retaliation as contained in Exod 21; Deut 19, and Lev 24. The law allowed a certain measure of revenge. While in later ages this law of private revenge became legally controlled by a court system and by legislation, it still tended to breathe something of the rancour of the old custom of "an eye for an eye" (Exod 21:24). Wisdom teaching hoped to refine this by introducing a moral tone, and an element of tolerance and control. In fact, v. 29 is a negative reformulation of the "golden rule" (20:22). Chapter 25:21 is the culmination of this morality: "if your enemy is hungry, give him bread to eat; if he is thirsty, give him water to drink".

All in all, this section forms a sapiential commentary on the *Tôrah,* viewing it from a more humane point of view. Verse 29 contains an implicit reminder that vengeance is the monopoly of the divinity, and that to arrogate his powers must surely be to the detriment of the whole community. There is a great deal in common between Law, Prophets and Sages when it comes to social justice, and in fact what Proverbs offers here is more an illustration of the commonly accepted idea. The sages' preoccupation with justice was to a degree due to the fact that *in practice* it is not always easy to define one's duty in the matter, and positively difficult to put it into practice. So certain steps are taken to clarify it. In the first place, it is not to be confused with charity or emotion, but implies strict impartiality. It never imposes on others, and indeed may often involve standing up for the rights of others (v. 25), even of enemies, and even to one's own detriment. It outlaws vengeance, inculcates truth and the rare quality of doing one's duty to self and to society, as well as is possible.

THE SLUGGARD. 24:30–34.

> [30] I passed by the field of a sluggard,
> by the vineyard of a man without sense;
> [31] and lo, it was all overgrown with thorns;
> the ground was covered with nettles,
> and its stone wall was broken down.
> [32] Then I saw and considered it;
> I looked and received instruction.
> [33] A little sleep, a little slumber,
> a little folding of the hands to rest,
> [34] and poverty will come upon you like a robber,
> and want like an armed man.

Here we have a semi-humorous portrait of the sluggard, in the same style as the portrait of the drunkard in chapter 23, and it is meant to underline the social necessity of hard work. It takes up once more, and sometimes in the same words, the theme of 6:9–11. Again, the personalized style is employed to press home the moral—not only does the sluggard belong in the same category as "the fool", he is risible, an object of mockery to the community. The scene is agrarian, dealing with agricultural life (v. 30), but the moral can as easily apply in the scribal school. It is this idea that points the moral. The *setting* may be a particular life-situation, the *parable* has universal application. *Walk while the daylight lasts.* Make use of the time and talents at your disposal, whatever be your avocation in life.

Book IV
The Collection of Proverbs Made for Hezekiah
25:1—29:27.

Wisdom Secular and Religious. 25:1—29:27.

Typical of a sophisticated editorial programme, these chapters present more of a unity than previous collections. The style moves from synthetic parallelism, represented by the juxtaposition of image and reality, to antithetic parallelism, represented by opposition of terms. Together, they form an integration of secular and religious, though perhaps to a more limited extent than heretofore.

The themes dealt with include the contrast of wise and fool, royal court, God and morality, human conduct and the structure of society. The first part, 25—27, represents the oldest tradition and the oldest wisdom formula for what is now called the doctrine of retribution, but should rather be seen as the theory of act and consequence. This is a semi-automatic connection, depending on the cosmic law identified with the will of Yahweh. It is concerned (or is for the most part) with the problems of everyday life. It most closely approaches the Egyptian and Mesopotamian cosmologies. The second part, 28—29, emphasizes more the role of Yahweh. In both sections there is an interest shown in social behaviour and its value for the individual. One who acts wisely is seen to have a constructive influence on society, diffusing well-being and prosperity in his community, while the fool injures himself, and plays a devisive role.

THE VOCATION OF GOVERNMENT. 25:1–7a.

The title "men of Hezekiah" is probably a reference to the professional scribes of the court of the king, or his personal writing staff. Hezekiah seems to have been almost a second Solomon, though on a smaller scale. With no political rivals, and no opposing king in the northern kingdom of Israel, he had the leisure to set about strengthening and centralizing learning in Judah. This sets its mark on the style of what follows.

25 These also are proverbs of Solomon which the men of Hezekiah
king of Judah copied.

[2]It is the glory of God to conceal things,
but the glory of kings is to search things out.
[3]As the heavens for height, and the earth for depth,
so the mind of kings is unsearchable.
[4]Take away the dross from the silver,
and the smith has material for a vessel;
[5]take away the wicked from the presence of the king,
and his throne will be established in righteousness.
[6]Do not put yourself forward in the king's presence
or stand in the place of the great;
[7]for it is better to be told, "Come up here,"
than to be put lower in the presence of the prince.

The preoccupation is similar to that of Book III. It takes up a common theme, the duty or "character" of the king, or the ruler (see 8:15; 14:28–35; 16:10–15; 19:12; 20:2; 22:11, 29 and 24:21). Once again, the actual political scene is indeterminate. It is not that of the people of Israel as such, so it is probably meant to be a common denominator for "ruler" or government, of whatever specific kind. This form of abstraction is a common sapiential device. The rest of the passage, vv. 2–7, presents an antithesis of God and king, religion and statecraft, and the analogous task of balancing the knowable and the mysterious. While the secular note is dominant, there is also the feeling here that religion, and the unsearchable character of the divine, are also elements with which the ruler will have to cope. The antithesis brings out one basic principle: while the things of God are inscrutable, the same is not true for the ruler. He may arrive at his policies by ways unknown to the people, but what he decides on must be comprehensible. Success in politics means getting to the bottom of human affairs. Wisdom thus becomes an agent in the service of government.

God's work is mysterious and transcendent, but it is the ruler's task to take in hand all the affairs of state, and to convince his people of the rightness of his administration. There must be no "secret government". This first insight may have been influenced by the actual historical situation, but there is little doubt that the sages saw it as universally applicable to government: "the glory of kings is to search things out" is grammatically an open statement (v. 2b), the king contrasted to God (v. 2a). Unlike God's sovereignty which remains transcendent, the policy of the king should be comprehensible (v. 2b), even though the subject may not know all that goes on in the making of policy (v. 3). Underhand dealings, or a paternalistic attitude of "the ruler knows best", is never acceptable in government. Yet there is a practical recognition of the fact that politics do have ramifications that the private individual is not always competent to grasp—"the mind of kings is unsearchable" is the antithesis presented by v. 3. It would therefore be unrealistic to think that politics can always be directed according to the whim of the ordinary citizen. Frequently he is neither competent nor knowledgeable. It also follows that the ruler himself must be capable, he must know what is going on, and must be of an enquiring and judicial nature—such is the meaning of *haqar,* "searching out" in the Hebrew text of v. 2. Ignorance on his part can only encourage political corruption (vv. 4–5). The sages are remarkably practical when it comes to politics.

Again, lack of communication, and an uninformed public, can breed personal corruption on the part of a ruler, with indifference and an abdication of personal responsibility on the part of the citizen—here v. 5 repeats the perception of 16:12. There is a consequent need in public affairs of personal integrity in a ruler, and a willingness to be advised according to a standard of "wisdom" (vv. 4–5). All governments are in their way despotic, but equity lies in their being "enlightened". Linguistically, v. 4 is somewhat unnatural; and this emphasises the point that the ruler is to some extent passive—he "can be purified", and the counsellor is to some extent active—"taking away wickedness from the king". In assigning posts in government service preference should go by ability and competence, and not by personal influence or favouritism. The counsellor should seek to be good, and not just well-known—certainly not one who puts himself "forward in the king's presence" (v. 6a), nor one who is put forward by his friends. The context is probably a banquet setting and personal preferment, but the whole meaning is nonetheless clear.

THE DANGERS OF GOSSIPING. 25:7b–10.

What your eyes have seen
[8] do not hastily bring into court;
for what will you do in the end,

when your neighbour puts you to
shame?
[9]Argue your case with your neighbour
himself,
and do not disclose another's
secret;
[10]lest he who hears you bring shame
upon you,
and your ill repute have no end.

Verse 7b begins with a straight warning against gossip—no matter whether the content be true or false—"whatever your eyes have seen", is the understood meaning of the text. And this is confirmed by "hastily" in v. 8, which certainly implies loose, thoughtless and therefore uncontrolled evidence. The motive is found in the sense of confusion and shame that the gossip feels as his foolish story is brought home to him (v. 8b), and he is revealed to all the community as an empty talker, and perhaps even one to be avoided. "Neighbour" must be taken, not in the narrow sense, but in the sense it usually has for the wisdom literature, where *re'a* signifies another human being. Human respect is the sanction once again.

The following verses present a parallel statement that reiterates, and so strengthens, the primary statement. If you *must* prattle, then discuss the matter with the person directly involved, in decent privacy, and do not bruit it abroad. Again, the sanction is clearly the opinion others are bound to have of you (v. 10). No-one can trust the compulsive raconteur: he is untrustworthy even when he means no harm, dangerous even, divisive. Verse 10b is subtly emphatic. The term "ill repute" is normally *active* in Hebrew, and concerns others. Here it is personalized to some advantage. "*Your* ill repute" suggests that it is a rebound; what you say of others to their detriment is precisely what they, and others, will end up saying about you. Once again, the sapiential interest in natural retribution comes to the surface.

Structurally, in fact, the emphasis lies on v. 9a: "argue

your case with your neighbour himself''; and this reveals the mind of the sage. As always when dealing with words and talk, what is advocated is a healthy, straightforward attitude and a recognition of the potency of words. Speak out, say what you have to say, and fear no reprisals. If it cannot be said to someone's face it *should* not be said. It is always wise to remember that no-one, not even you, has a monopoly on truth, knows all the facts, and can adequately interpret them (Kidner). And indeed the gossip's motives are seldom pure; so often they really reflect a sense of inadequacy, or even cowardice.

THE BOOK OF FOOLS. 26:1–12.

What follows is a series of short, sharp and exceedingly sarcastic comments on the fool and his works. They are almost perfect examples of the proverb type, each one is a unit in itself, the unifying factor being the subject matter rather than any natural sequence. The final verse is also the final word on folly.

> **26** Like snow in summer or rain in harvest,
> so honour is not fitting for a fool.
> [2]Like a sparrow in its flitting, like a swallow in its flying,
> a curse that is causeless does not alight.
> [3]A whip for the horse, a bridle for the ass,
> and a rod for the back of fools.
> [4]Answer not a fool according to his folly,
> lest you be like him yourself.
> [5]Answer a fool according to his folly,
> lest he be wise in his own eyes.
> [6]He who sends a message by the hand of a fool

cuts off his own feet and drinks
violence.
[7]Like a lame man's legs, which hang
useless,
is a proverb in the mouth of fools.
[8]Like one who binds the stone in the
sling
is he who gives honour to a fool.
[9]Like a thorn that goes up into the
hand of a drunkard
is a proverb in the mouth of fools.
[10]Like an archer who wounds
everybody
is he who hires a passing fool or
drunkard.
[11]Like a dog that returns to his vomit
is a fool that repeats his folly.
[12]Do you see a man who is wise in his
own eyes?
There is more hope for a fool than
for him.

The first verse begins with what to the sage would appear as a complete intellectual negative: "*honour* is not fitting for a fool". Such a one lacks honour, the quality most prized by the wise. Here it probably stands for public respect and the esteem of one's peers. It is always possible, especially in public life, for an incompetent or a fool to each high office, but the honour fits ill on such a person, and the effect is too often the mockery of society. There is a slight change in v. 2, which deals, not with the fool as such, but with the rash curse that such a person is likely to indulge in. The atmosphere is still folly. Taking the text at its immediate level, one observes that what is characteristic of the sparrow in its flight is aimlessness. And this characterizes the activity of the fool. Possibly the origin of the saying is to be found in a refutation of the older biblical concept of the inherent effectiveness of the curse, or the blessing. Here in the text, however, it is used as a metaphor of any foolish or fruitless activity. Indeed, the fool is no more than an animal that needs, and deserves, restraints other than reason (v. 3), for reason is wasted on such. The only way to talk to the fool is by means of language that can pierce his hide. And this remains outside logic. Each fool has his own folly and so needs his own answer. Verses 4–5, by using seemingly contradictory proverbs, leaves the answer to the reader, and at the same time emphasizes the uncontrollable aspect of folly. It is for this reason that vv. 4–5 is classically gnomic in style: "answer *not* a fool according to his folly . . ." is seemingly contradicted by "*answer* a fool according to his folly . . .", but then, faced with a fool, of what value is *any* statement? This antithesis may even imply that to try and answer a fool at all reduces one to the same level. And this may be confirmed by v. 6, which deals with the folly of one who sends a fool as a messenger—it is tantamount to sending no one at all, for it "cuts off one's feet", immobilizing the sender. The phrase as it stands in the text is obscure, but we must remember that it may be deliberately laconic. After all, with reference to a fool what *can* one say?

The short proverb that is v. 7 is almost art for art's sake—a proverb within a proverb. And so it is highly attractive. Since a proverb always depends on the perceptiveness of *both* author and reader, one that comes from "the mouth of a fool" is doubly fatuous: meaningless in its origin and its end. Verse 8 returns the reader to the example of the fool who achieves a measure of public status, and it is always possible that the author had a particular character in mind. However, the process is radically absurd, like spiking one's own gun before trying to shoot a target—"like one who *binds the stone* in a sling" (v. 8a). In sequence, v. 9 returns to the idea expressed by v. 7, a "proverb in the mouth of a fool"—an intellectual dead-end, proceeding from nowhere to nowhere. But a new element is added, a note of positive menace: it may be an absurdity, but it can nonetheless inflict hurt: those who are disposed to take it any way seriously may find it a "thorn that goes up into the hand of a drunkard" (v. 9a). It may look funny, but it is not funny to the one who is on the receiving end!

Whatever unity is contained in this section appears under the banner of v. 12: "a man who is wise in his own eyes" says it all. All truth contains an element of the inscrutable, evades our total comprehension. This is recognized by the scribes as the "nature of things". Thus only the uncritical, the naive, the *peta'îm* of the Book of Proverbs, would take anything in life to be clear and unequivocal, and thus think he could measure all—his own ideas, the ideas of others, the way life goes—and measure them *adequately* against his own experience. Such a one is not receptive enough for *any* experience to have a free range to manoeuvre. Thus v. 12 adds the key to the moral content of the section. Much of human folly, as seen in vv. 1–11, may be risible, but there is nothing whatever funny about the summit of foolishness—that self-conceit that closes one's mind to any hope of learning. A "man wise in his own eyes" has nothing to achieve and nowhere to go. Life has nothing left to offer.

ON HYPOCRISY. 26:23–28.

[23] Like the glaze covering an earthen vessel
are smooth lips with an evil heart.
[24] He who hates, dissembles with his lips
and harbours deceit in his heart;
[25] when he speaks graciously, believe him not,
for there are seven abominations in his heart;
[26] though his hatred be covered with guile,

his wickedness will be exposed in
the assembly.
[27] He who digs a pit will fall into it,
and a stone will come back upon
him who starts it rolling.
[28] A lying tongue hates its victims,
and a flattering mouth works ruin.

In a way, the first verse of this short pericope on truth and lies says all there is to say: "the *glaze* covering an *earthen* vessel". This was a rich image to contemporaries. A porus vessel of thrown clay cannot be used to hold oil or water in a household, so it has no real utility. A mere coating of glaze may give it a superficial usefulness but in no way changes its nature as raw earthenware. It is first necessary for the vessel to be fired, and a chemical change brought about, before it can be of use. The glazing may make the raw earth *look* finished, but it is of no real value. The image is visual, rather than conceptual. Verse 25 combines with the previous verses to form a literary unit, and indeed furnishes the moral. "Gracious speaking" is worth precisely what the intention of "the heart" is worth. Here there is at least a suggestion of morality, the term "abominations" in Proverbs normally having a religious significance. It is possible that here we have, once more, a sapiential re-interpretation of *tôrah* religion, of truth as an aspect of faith. In v. 26 "assembly" should not be taken in an exclusive, or cultic, sense: it means any community of people. The social sanction is what is in question here, as it was for example in 25:7–10. This is a normal agent of "retribution" in the more secular passages of the book. But here the broader meaning should be maintained. One's influence on the community, and one's value for good, is commensurate with one's integrity and honesty.

Verse 27 confirms this idea by returning to the concept of natural retribution: the person's own works and words contain within them a natural dynamism, and the effect will recoil upon the speaker himself: he has "dug a pit", his words have created something with a life of its own, and he may so easily "fall into it" himself. As is usual with these short collections of proverbial material, the last verse serves as a summary to the thinking of the sages. Verse 28 may therefore be taken as a conclusion to this pericope: "a lying tongue hates its victims, and a flattering mouth works ruin". Two parallel stichoi, that lays the emphasis on the words "works ruin". This is a destructive act. It may refer equally to the effect of a loose tongue on the victim (v. 28a) or on the possessor himself. The emphasis would seem to be on the latter idea, the concept of natural retribution. One creates one's own ambient, makes one's own bed.

Speech was an important aspect of human life for the sages. The search for wisdom is a worthy enterprise, and one finds it among the wise on the lips and in the heart of an intelligent person. By meeting such people, and listening to their speech we also may acquire wisdom. But we must avoid those who misuse mind and tongue (see 10:31; 13:20; 14:7). Truthfulness in every dimension of life is the result of a basic honesty, to the extent that even a brutal honesty in speech is better than any form of lying or deceit.

ON FRIENDSHIP. 27:8–10.

[8]Like a bird that strays from its nest,
is a man who strays from his
home.
[9]Oil and perfume make the heart glad,
but the soul is torn by trouble.
[10]Your friend, and your father's
friend, do not forsake;
and do not go to your brother's
house in the day of your
calamity.
Better is a neighbour who is near
than a brother who is far away.

The first verse of this short section (v. 8) establishes the principle that is loosely worked out in the following verses. "Home" here in translation is, in the Hebrew text, "one's own place", and it is therefore a general, and not a local designation. It can mean one's home, or one's native land, or—more probably given the present context—one's natural or chosen ambient. What is particularly in question is the *human* ambient—family, friends or community. The language is deliberately general, so it is probably a question of alienation from one's proper human environment, the community. Verse 9 is a true proverb, an induced similarity between dissimilar things. "Oil and perfume" (v. 9a) are purveyors of sensual pleasure, whereas the "soul" (v. 9b) stands for spiritual pleasure, which, given the context, is friendship. The Hebrew text as it stands now is obscure, but it clearly speaks of the "sweetness of a friend". Perhaps a better translation of v. 9 would be—"oil and incense rejoice one's heart, and so does the sweetness of a friend's support". In misfortune, there is nothing more agreeable than the loyalty and warmth of human friendship: one can really *feel* it as one might the application of a soothing oil.

Verse 10 may, if taken too literally, present a problem, for it deals with three disparate examples of friendship: a family friend, a relation and a neighbour. Perhaps the key to interpretation is to be found in 10b—"in the day of your calamity". It is in time of need that friendship shows its true colours, and indeed gives most consolation. In tragic circumstances it can most truly be said that "no man is an island". This may be borne out by the internal antithesis of v. 10c, a friend "who is near" and a blood-relation who is careful to keep himself "far away". Friendship essentially resides in *deeds,* not in formulae of consanguinity. There lies a great deal of practical experience behind the stark statement of 10b and 10c: "do not go to your brother's house in the day of your calamity", for "better is a neighbour who is near than a brother who is far away".

The "friend" is not as dominant a figure in Proverbs as is

the "parent", the "ruler" or the "fool", but he is close to the heart of the sage. There is no doubt that his first characteristic is *loyalty.* A relation may have closer natural ties, but can often let one down badly—"there are friends who pretend to be friends, but there is a friend who sticks closer than a brother" (18:24). A "client" stays close, but only as long as one is successful and prominent—once you can no longer be of use to him he finds something to do elsewhere (14:20; 19:4–9). Constancy, and neither propinquity nor declarations of fidelity, is what marks out the real friend (v. 10a). But while friendship is ready to *give,* it also makes *demands,* and one must remain loyal. It is this sharp, double-edged perception that is dominant here in Prov 27, for v. 10c can apply both ways.

ON SOCIAL RESPONSIBILITY. 27:11–14.

[11] Be wise, my son, and make my heart glad,
that I may answer him who reproaches me.
[12] A prudent man sees danger and hides himself;
but the simple go on, and suffer for it.
[13] Take a man's garment when he has given surety for a stranger,
and hold him in pledge when he gives surety for foreigners.
[14] He who blesses his neighbour with a loud voice,
rising early in the morning,
will be counted as cursing.

With v. 11 we return to the parent/child formula of earlier collections, and the teaching concern here is success in life and in society. "Wise" in v. 11a is a general admonition, and normal human sagacity is what is in question.

Success is important to both teacher and pupil, for it is often a gauge of goodness. The "reproach" feared by the teacher is public recognition of his failure to lead the pupil to success and prosperity in life.

Verse 13 is an illustration of the principle enunciated in the previous verse, and in 20:16. Prudence is a quality that recognises the social, or community, effect of one's actions. To give one's garment in pledge (v. 13) was a common gesture in Israelite society, "garment" being the usual surety offered by one who asked for a loan (as in Deut 24:10–13). It might be kept if the loan were not repaid. For a fellow Israelite one was expected not to apply the law too strictly, as stated in Exod 22:25: "If you lend money to any of my people with you who is poor, you should not be to him as a creditor". With strangers one should be more strict, for such people have no roots in the community. Thus to give surety for "a stranger" is irresponsible, for it leaves the community liable to loss if the outsider defaults. Given the close-knit, almost tribal, circumstances in which many of this type of proverb were written, it is less narrow-minded an injunction than may appear to later ages, and community life and independance could be precarious. Even in changed circumstances the basic principle applies—be wary of a generous gesture that others may have to pay for. The point of view is practical. Generosity is an open gesture, and one gives outright of one's own without counting the cost (22:9), but making a loan is always a gamble, and the risk increases with outsiders. The sages well knew that making loans easily bred bad feeling—on the part of the donor, who loses his investment; of the community, who may have to make up the loss; and even of the recipient, who may dislike the feeling of being beholden (see 6:1–5; 20:16; 22:27).

Verse 14 is a condemnation of public hypocrisy—the loud-voiced praise of someone who may be of use in the future: "early in the morning", as it is used in Hebrew, underlines the exaggerated nature of the "praise", which does little good to the object of such adulation, for everyone knows its value, and one might just as well be cursed as praised in this futile way.

THE NEED FOR A PERSONAL STANDARD OF VALUES. 28:1–13.

The vocabulary of wisdom is used in a new way so as to develop a new kind of piety—the search for God which is also the search for moral discernment. Thus *Tôrah* becomes, in this chapter, more the divine instruction than the teaching of the sage.

28 The wicked flee when no one
pursues,
but the righteous are bold as a lion.
[2]When a land transgresses
it has many rulers;
but with men of understanding and
knowledge
its stability will long continue.
[3]A poor man who oppresses the poor
is a beating rain that leaves no
food.
[4]Those who forsake the law praise the
wicked,
but those who keep the law strive
against them.
[5]Evil men do not understand justice,
but those who seek the Lord
understand it completely.
[6]Better is a poor man who walks in
his integrity
than a rich man who is perverse
in his ways.
[7]He who keeps the law is a wise son,
but a companion of gluttons
shames his father.

[8]He who augments his wealth by
interest and increase
gathers it for him who is kind to
the poor.
[9]If one turns away his ear from hearing
the law,
even his prayer is an abomination.
[10]He who misleads the upright into
an evil way
will fall into his own pit;
but the blameless will have a
goodly inheritance.
[11]A rich man is wise in his own eyes,
but a poor man who has understanding will find him out.
[12]When the righteous triumph, there is
great glory;
but when the wicked rise, men hide
themselves.
[13]He who conceals his transgressions
will not prosper,
but he who confesses and forsakes
them will obtain mercy.

This establishes the basic principle, dear to the wisdom teachers and crucial to their thought: the first requisite for human conduct is conscience, for this leads to security and even confidence. From this one can walk confidently on any path. In keeping with the basic antithesis, the impious are seen as feeling insecure, because they *are,* fundamentally, insecure, having no anchor-chain.

Socially, this can be seen in politics, for the first result of good conscience is a stable government. At the root of all political upheaval lies some form of social corruption, for justice breeds justice, and a ruler who acts according to enlightened conscience is also likely to have the courage of his convictions. With their own distinctive way of looking at things, the sages saw that social consequences normally arise more from the *nature* or character of the wise or foolish ones than from their *conduct.* Moral aberrance is almost invariably the result of an unformed conscience or of plain ignorance (v. 4): "those who foresake the law" are those whose conscience is dead. The general idea of these first verses seems to be that ignorance, allied to a lack of personal standards of conduct, results inevitably in social injustice and its consequence, political upheaval. The solution to the problem of social unrest is not always found in first changing social *conditions;* frequently it is more effective to change the values and standards by which individuals govern. One normally associates political oppression with the rich and powerful, but it is not really their prerogative, though it most often happens that way. The powerful tend to be ignorant of what it means to be oppressed, and this can leave the underdog with some residual dignity; but oppression by a member of one's own class—by someone who, knowing what it implies, oppresses his own kind—is far more degrading (v. 3).

Changing over to the individual effects of good conscience, v. 5b repeats the principle. It is first necessary to establish a well-formed conscience, knowledge of God's ways and his will, and on that basis come to an understanding of the personal implications of justice. One's own integrity is the first, the fundamental, priority in life and it must become the quality that determines all (v. 6). The only influence that keeps one "on the right way" is a knowledge of abstract truth, and its practical application. This is seen in the way the "wicked" *actually* turn aside from the way, and examples of this are given in vv. 8–10. The warning against loans in v. 8 may now appear overspeculative, but in context it was realistic, and it illustrates a principle that the sage wishes to teach. Loans were habitually made to poor people, not for them to use for investment purposes, or to produce a profit, but to enable them to acquire the basic necessities of life. That was the predominant reason people had for borrowing, so to demand interest was in fact to *exploit* the needs of other human beings for one's own gain; effectively, to *use* others as if they were *things,* not people.

A warning is spoken here to the rich. Affluence is a recognized good in itself, no sage would deny that; but it undoubtedly tends to make its possessor far too self-confident and inclined to equate riches and wisdom, as if the mere possession of wealth were in itself a human quality. Ultimately, it is this *quality* in one's life that stands to one as of real value. It is a sapiential insight that even if an upright man remains poor, he has integrity (vv. 6, 8, 11). Verse 6 stated the principle: "better a poor man walking in integrity". This is an interesting use of "integrity" (Hebrew *tumah*), for it suggests the possession of *spiritual* wealth, a human wholeness that money cannot bring. In this context, and this is emphasized by the following verses, moral riches and poverty seem to set off in contrast material riches and poverty. Nor is wealth necessarily a concomitant of impiety (as some poor might like to think); to use it generously, for good, is righteousness. This is a wisdom re-interpretation of the law of retribution, where wealth and success tend to be synonymous with righteousness, and poverty with wickedness.

The truly wise person is one who seeks God and the things of God, and if riches accrue that is over and above. It is clear that here we have more than a wisdom instruction. We have also a new insight into the problem of theodicy: the rich may be morally poor, the poor may have a moral wealth, and having it have also a security and a quality of life denied the materially wealthy.

ON INDUSTRY ALLIED TO INTEGRITY. 28:19–22.

[19] He who tills his land will have
plenty of bread,
but he who follows worthless
pursuits will have plenty of
poverty.
[20] A faithful man will abound with
blessings,
but he who hastens to be rich will

not go unpunished.
[21] To show partiality is not good;
but for a piece of bread a man
will do wrong.
[22] A miserly man hastens after wealth,
and does not know that want will
come upon him.

Antithetic parallelism dominates this series of proverbs. Verse 19 is a more directly stated version of 12:11. The immediate setting is rural, and the suggestion is that one who is diligent in the pursuit of his avocation will prosper. Given the Hebrew style of the verse, the antithesis between 19a and 19b places the emphasis, not on the result of hard work, but on the *way* one approaches one's tasks. "Worthless pursuits" is a reference to a lack of purpose, rather than to idleness. One's activity must be directed. Verse 20 speaks of trustworthiness, that is, fidelity to one's word on the practical level—in commerce, in social obligations, in applying oneself to one's tasks. This is the bedrock of social and community life. It is clear that the author is distrustful of those who "hasten to be rich" (in 20b and again in 22a), for people who have such a craving to "get rich quick" tend to cut too many corners, even unconsciously, and so gradually will fall into dishonest practices: negative evil—"worthless pursuits", leading to positive wickedness. The sages always had their eyes on the possible consequences of dishonesty—or folly!

The change of context in v. 21 underlines and expands this concern, by changing the circumstances to a court of law, where even a small illegality—favouring a friend, perhaps (21a), accepting a trifling handout (21b)—may lead further than anyone wants to go, a perception found also in 6:26. The short pericope on assiduity and integrity ends, in typical sapiential style, with a positive statement, strongly drawn: v. 22 speaks of an outright, genuinely bad person: "a miserly man hastens after wealth". The antithetic structure serves to add colour to the picture, the passage from plenty ("wealth") to "want": and since in all practicality the miser seldom becomes materially poor, the idea of a state of "want" may need to be reinterpreted. He keeps his wealth, such as it is, but progressively becomes "lacking" in what is of real value. An avaricious man is naturally unsympathetic, self-seeking. The text of v. 22 describes him as "evil of eye" ("miserly" in the RSV translation)—an unusual term in Proverbs, used elsewhere only in 23:6 (where the RSV translates it as "stingy"), and it brings to mind the antithesis "good of eye", that is, benevolent and open. Both positive and negative terms are used in the context of social intercourse. They refer to the way one regards others, the way one deals with one's fellow human beings.

ON PROBITY. 29:1–3.

In this last chapter of Book IV the traditional equation of righteousness and its reward, wickedness and its due punishment returns and in its own way dominates the teaching.

29 He who is often reproved, yet
stiffens his neck,
will suddenly be broken beyond
healing.
[2]When the righteous are in authority,
the people rejoice;
but when the wicked rule, the
people groan.
[3]He who loves wisdom makes his
father glad,
but one who keeps company with
harlots squanders his substance.

The term used here in v. 1—"stiffens his neck"—is interesting. It is the direct antithesis of "bending the neck", the due token of submission to a superior or ruler. So what is in question is the attitude of *stubborn* persistence, beyond anything that might justifiably be called for. Such a one will naturally "be broken, and suddenly", and the sharpness of the statement makes the reader think again about the meaning of v. 1. What precisely is the cause of this act of breaking? It can only be either a divine intervention or a social sanction imposed by a human agency. Given the secular context, it is probably the latter, and we are dealing with a natural and inevitable reaction. The idea has already been dealt with in a more picturesque way in 1:24–26.

Folly, the antithesis of wisdom, takes many forms, and in v. 3 it appears as licentious living, a life ruled only by pleasure. Again, the result of human activity is described in interesting terms: such a one "squanders his substance". This is not merely material substance, but the essential value of human life, and so v. 3 in its way contains the same teaching as Ps 1—the life of the fool is as ephemeral as chaff that is blown away. The second verse is a variant of this "law" of natural retribution. Here the idea of retribution focuses on the social value of human activity.

ON PEACEMAKERS. 29:8–11.

[8]Scoffers set a city aflame,
but wise men turn away wrath.
[9]If a wise man has an argument with
a fool,
the fool only rages and laughs,
and there is no quiet.
[10]Bloodthirsty men hate one who is
blameless,
and the wicked seek his life.
[11]A fool gives full vent to his anger,
but a wise man quietly holds it
back.

A subject close to the interests of the wisdom teachers was the constructive and creative role each individual can play in society. Such is that of peacemaking. Here in four verses the type is characterized. A "scoffer" (v. 8) is a loose-living, irresponsible type who has no interest in moral obligations to the community or to others, and so leaves everyone else angry at him, and out of sorts. Scoffing is not, as such, a positive attitude of wickedness, but refers to what might be called moral flippancy. It is a personal rather than a social disease. To pillory such might seem somewhat petty, but given the actual state of human society it is the small, irksome thorn-in-the-flesh that is most disruptive. This verse shows that concern for everyday life that typifies Proverbs. The wise go quietly about their tasks, and by such normal and unobtrusive service oil the wheels of society and make peaceful cohabitation possible. Verse 9 returns to the idea of the fool, and by extension the folly of anyone who tries to have practical dealings with such. It is certainly no sign of wisdom to enter into public controversy with someone whose reaction is likely to be irrational, who "rages and laughs" (v. 9b). The end result is turmoil, emotional discomfort and noise. The fool blusters in public, lacks balance, has no sense of what is due in a situation, and ends up making more intelligent people as disturbed as himself. Nothing profitable can come from such an encounter. A calm, quiet approach is best when possible, and otherwise a certain aloofness, a dignified refusal to indulge in histrionics, or to suffer those of others.

Verse 10 carries on the logic of v. 9, by reversing the coin and giving an illustration of the effect on the fool that the wise person's control has.

Verse 11 sums up in one word the wisdom of 29:8–11—restraint. The word used for "anger" in the Masoretic Text of 11a is *ruach,* "spirit, mind", and suggests the whole personality. "Letting it all out" would perhaps be a better contemporary translation. The fool is one who has no constraints, no reserve. "Holds it back" in 11b may refer to the anger of the fool in 11a, suggesting that the wise can control the excesses of the fool; but given the structure of the verse in Hebrew it is more likely the wise person's *own* wrath that is restrained, as indeed the Greek Septuagint version brings out. Going by the antithetic parallelism, the better translation would be: "the fool gives full vent to his anger, but the wise person restrains his anger and remains calm".

Thus the true peacemaker in a community is not seen as a particularly charismatic figure, or a leader. He is an ordinary person who controls himself, his emotions, his reactions. In cases of conflagration, a wet-blanket is useful. The natural attitude would be to react against folly, against what offends personal standards, but the wise realizes that this serves little real purpose when one is faced with a fool in his folly. It is far better not to react at all.

ON THE FAMILY. 29:15–17.

> [15] The rod and reproof give wisdom,
> but a child left to himself brings
> shame to his mother.
> [16] When the wicked are in authority,
> transgression increases;
> but the righteous will look upon
> their downfall.
> [17] Discipline your son, and he will give
> you rest;
> he will give delight to your heart.

Verse 15 takes up the double concept of discipline and education common to this particular book, but introduces a small though interesting note of change.

"The rod and reproof" are instruments of training. A child left to its own devices is a shameful waste, a talent untapped. The function of discipline is positive: its aim is to foster strong character and develop personal gifts (see 7:3), which will enable the young person to achieve a full life. However, and this is an idea taken up again in v. 17, the rod is not to become its own end. Proverbs always sees this form of discipline in terms of a school or a family, and is respectful of both institutions. Together, parents (or teachers) and children find fulfillment with each other (see 17:6). The attitude of vv. 15 and 17 may appear hard, but it is the practical expression of a definite philosophy. The child is by nature unformed, or "foolish", and it takes more than good example alone to form such a one; discipline is essential, and if the parent or teacher does not give it, life will (v. 15b). The young are by nature resilient, and susceptible to training. Pain fades quickly from their memory, as long as it is not associated with cruelty or whim.

What is interesting here is the mention of only one parent, and the obvious lack of strain in mentioning only the mother. This aspect of v. 15 may be a linguistic device, to bring a little variety to the usual parent/child, teacher/pupil style, but this is unlikely, given the scattered and amorphous nature of the proverbs in chapter 29. It is more likely to be a recognition of the primary role of the mother in the education of the child *in basic human values,* before the teacher or father takes over on the technical level. It also reflects the general attitude of Proverbs. In this book both parents share the basic responsibility for educating and rearing children, this has already been seen in Prov 1:8–9; 6:20; etc. Possibly because of its emphasis on education, and its individualist tendency, woman plays an important role in wisdom literature, especially with regard to the family and to education. Emphasis on this aspect of life led the sages to an appreciation of monogamy, and exalted the position of women to equality. For example, 31:1–9 makes it quite clear how central the influence of the mother was on the formation and education of a young person for life. Certainly a parity in spheres of influence is in question.

In v. 16 the antithetic structure suggests that good example, and indeed good government in any sphere, will inevitably influence the life of the subject or the pupil. Verse 17 is almost an inclusion, rounding off this section on the family with a return to the mutual relationship of respect and love, of care and warmth that marks the ideal family. There is seldom in these texts a reference to material prosperity.

Book V
Four Appendices
30:1—31:31.

APPENDICES
30:1—31:31

The last two chapters of the Book of Proverbs consist of a variety of writings on a number of disparate subjects. The style is clearly different to what has gone before, 30—31 probably being a later redactional effort added here as a form of general conclusion to the whole book. In structure, it is composed of four appendices.

The Words of Agur. 30:1–9.
Numerical Proverbs and Sayings. 30:10–33.
The Words of Lemuel. 31:1–9.
The Woman beyond Price. 31:10–31.

Both chapters begin with the phrase "of Massa" (30:1 and 31:1) embedded in the title. While this may be taken as a geographic designation, Massa being a tribal region in the Arabian peninsula known from Gen 25:14 and 1 Chr 1:30, it is more likely to be a stylistic device linking the two chapters. In Hebrew, the word "massa" can mean an oracle, or other solemn statement, and this may be intended to mark the final group of appendices according to the mind of the editor.

Appendix 1: The Words of Agur. 30:1–9.

Chapter 30 is difficult to classify, as it consists of a number of unrelated sections, differing in scope and in style. It is probably quite late. The title supplied in v. 1 is "words of Agur", but this scarcely applies to the whole chapter, for the style changes in v. 10. It is more likely that the first nine verses contain the actual "words" of Agur, and the rest of the chapter contains a series of separate sections including numerical proverbs and admonitions.

DIALOGUE OF A SCEPTIC AND A BELIEVER. 30:1–9.

[1]The words of Agur son of Jakeh,
a solemn statement.

The saying of the man who has
no god;
I have no god, but I can do without.
[2]For I am too stupid to be a man,
nor have I the understanding
of a man.
[3]I have not learned wisdom,
nor have I knowledge
of the divinity.
[4]Who is it that has gone up
to the heavens, and come
down again? Who has gathered
the wind in his fists?
Who has wrapped up the waters
in a mantle? Who has
established the ends of the
earth?
What is his name, and what the
name of his son?
Surely you know!
[5]Every word of the Lord
has been refined.
He is a shield to those
who trust in him.
[6]Do not add to his words, lest

he rebuke you, and you
be found a liar.
[7]Two things I request from you,
do not withhold them
from me before I die:
[8]Keep falsehood and lying
far from me;
give me neither poverty nor
riches;
but only my due portion
of bread to eat.
[9]Lest being sated I deny you, and say
"Who is the Lord?";
lest being poor I steal,
and profane the name of my God.

(*translation by the author*)

Who is Agur? Some authors take Massa to be a proper name, the region mentioned in Gen 25, in which case Agur is non-Israelite, a foreigner with a foreign point of view. Probably, therefore, he is one of those represented by the term "enemies" in the psalms, or the "fools" who tend to see God as an aloof, uninterested divinity. Others take "massa" as a form of the word *mashal,* proverb, in which case we are dealing with a gnomic utterance, or a solemn statement. In spite of the exegetes, Agur maintains his anonymity, and so qualifies to stand with Job as representative of a widely-held point of view—a deep-seated scepticism.

"Saying" (*ne'um*) invariably introduces the direct oracle or saying, so v. 1a is a *title* for what follows in three parts. The text of 1b is obscure, and the translation most often found—"The man says to Ithiel, to Ithiel and Ukal"—scarcely makes sense. Others translate it as an ejaculation addressed to God: as for example "I am weary, O God, I am weary." However, in v. 3 the author disclaims any knowledge of God, so it is unlikely that this first verse could be addressed to the divinity. Accepting the Masoretic Text as the basis for analysis, and making a very few minor alterations in the *spacing* of the consonants, and in the vowel signs (a later addition), one can come up with a possible, and intelligible translation of v. 1b. The text at first sight reads "to ithiel, to ithiel and ukal", in Hebrew *le'îtî'el, le'îtî'el we'ukal.* Slightly modified, this can read *lo 'ito 'el* (who has no God), *lo 'iti 'el* (I have no God), *we'ukal* (and I am able . . .). The justification for the first phrase (who has no God) is found in the fact that the same grammatical structure is used to the same end elsewhere in the Hebrew text of the Old Testament (Jer 8:8; Prov 8:18 and 11:2), and indeed the Vulgate puts it positively—"the man to whom God is present". The second phrase is a variant of this, with 3rd person changed to 1st person. The final phrase takes the word to be an Imperfect *Qal* (indicative) form of the verb "to be able" (*yakal*), found also in other Old Testament texts (cf. Isa 1:13 and Ps 101:5). Thus v. 1b is a statement of principle—Agur is not a believer, or at least expresses positive scepticism about the presence of God, and to him this is no great inconvenience.

The second verse begins with the word *kî,* "for", which serves to introduce a motive clause, which follows in vv. 2–4 as the speaker gives the reason for his open scepticism. Verse 2 is an ironic, indeed almost an openly sarcastic, reaction to the claims of the "wise", the believers: "naturally, you clever people know it all, and have grasped the mystery of God, but I am poor and simple". A little heavy-handed, perhaps, but effective. For the author of "Agur", the mystery of God is not so easily penetrated. He claims not to have the discernment others seem to have. Like Job, which this passage resembles, there is a scepticism regarding traditional theology. This claimed, particularly in its more conventional moments, to see God as a ruling power behind human affairs, an idea possibly reflected in the following section—vv. 5–9. Agur has never been able to penetrate this domain of knowledge. Search as he may, God remains hidden. In v. 3 the term "holy ones" is used. This is a usage common to the Old Testament (as for instance its use already in Prov 9:10), the so-called plural of majesty. It means God himself, the divinity. Verse 4 gets to the heart of the problem with the question, "what is his name?" In Hebrew thought *shem,* name, signifies the essence of something, the nature of someone; and one cannot know this without the possession of the name (see Gen 32:29; Exod 3:13; Isa 52:6). The addition of "the name of his son" is poetic parallelism, like that found in Ps 8:4, and it is meant to underline the fact that one really can *know* nothing about God. Knowledge comes from experience, as the sages well knew, and who can be said to have experienced God? This is brought out by the continued irony of the final words in v. 4—"surely *you* know", you so wise people. Only those who have actually gone up to the heavens can speak of the nature of the heavens; only those who have seen God can accept him as a reality. Thus, the traditional faith in the "Lord", claimed by conventional sages, lacks the empiric basis, the basis in experience, central to wisdom thinking. To the protagonist of vv. 1–4 God, if he exists at all, certainly remains hidden, inaccessible to human research. The knowledge of God spoken of so confidently in the tradition has no empiric basis, and is unworthy of rational human beings. All of this is reminiscent of Job and the attitude of its author: see for example Job 38:1–38; 40:4; 42:2–6. To this sort of argument the tradition can, of course, present an answer. God, it will say, can and does transcend human reason and man's limited experience. Agur knows this, and precludes such specious argumentation by recourse to the basic theological principle of the sapiential tradition. God has given mankind the gift of mind and reason, or so it is said (the basic teaching of the Priestly Tradition). In that case the sages who would uphold divine transcendence against the claims of human intelligence are, as Agur sarcastically recalls, deserting their own academic principles, the alliance of experience and reason.

The next two verses, 5–6, seem to present the traditional

answer. The style changes now from scepticism to faith, and the images change accordingly. The language used in these verses is taken, almost without change, from the tradition: Deut 4:2; 2 Sam 22:31; Pss 12:6 and 18:30. Verse 5b is certainly typical psalmic style. Here, then, we find the answer of faith: that God is supreme, that his revelation must be accepted, for it embodies truth, and infidelity or disbelief can only end in tribulation. This represents the response of the most conservative school of yahwistic faith, and differs so obviously from the point of view of the sages. Yet it is by no means treated unsympathetically. There is no irony here, as in vv. 2–4. Rather, faith is presented in wholesome terms, as a personal relationship with God, as an intimacy with and confidence in the divinity that can carry one beyond reason. There is no effort made here to coerce the reader's allegiance; neither argument is forced, both sides are carefully presented—scepticism and faith — and one may (and indeed *should*) honestly choose between them. There is clearly a problem of reason, no one denies that; and "faith" can too often be a blind credulity. The answer given in vv. 5–6 seems to express a confidence that God has somehow revealed himself by his word, in his actions, and can therefore in some way be experienced. Yet one may never pretend; faith remains an option that is basically a-rational, and in rational eyes this must always be its weakness. It may have been the intention of the author of vv. 5–6 to put vv. 1–4 into perspective, but it is as likely that the first verses supply the rational perspective for faith.

As they stand, vv. 5–6 present the traditional answer of faith. Knowledge of God must be founded on a relationship of faith, and not solely on reason. Faith has its own particular conviction, arguments that appear no less determinative to the believer. God will always remain a mystery, to believer and unbeliever alike. However, the basic encounter with him need not be less *real* for all that it transcends the human intellect. It can nonetheless pertain to the realm of "experience", and one can rejoice in his presence even if he remains a "hidden God". Even here the wisdom categories retain a certain validity, for one can attain a perception of "his words" (the dominant phrase in these two verses) by means of docility, openness and discipline.

There follows, in vv. 7–9, a prayer that illuminates the author's concept of discipline, and that stands as a personal defence against the scepticism of vv. 1–4. The request found here is simple—and classic: the strength to shun falsehood of any kind, and protection from any element of excess. This prayer is similar to that offered by Job in 13:20, though there the tone is far more personal, as if the problem of faith and reason had got under the skin of the author and become a cancer. Proverbs remains more detached, looking to a life without extremes as a bulwark of security. This whole section is dominated by a certain strain of intellectual independence and abstraction, which suggests that it may be more a textbook exercise of "for and against" than a real effort at grappling with a problem.

Appendix 2:
Numerical Proverbs and Sayings. 30:10–33.

The rest of this chapter is given over to a collection of well-written, and clearly thought out, proverbs and sayings. There is no particular inner unity, unless it be the classic binary structure common to the pure proverb form, and what seems to be a pervasive interest in the mysterious dimension of human life, the inexplicable, and therefore the perennially fascinating to the thinker and the poet.

THE FOURTH WONDERFUL THING. 30:18–20.

[18] Three things are too wonderful for
me;
four I do not understand:

[19] the way of an eagle in the sky,
the way of a serpent on a rock,
the way of a ship on the high seas,
and the way of a man with a
maiden.

[20] This is the way of an adulteress:
she eats, and wipes her mouth,
and says, "I have done no wrong."

In form this, like most of the numerical proverbs, resembles the onomasticon much used internationally by writers of the sapiential tradition, but here the purpose is *not* to control nature, nor is it an instrument of classification. Wonder, and a graceful acknowledgement of the mystery that surrounds life, breathes through these verses.

This is emphasized by the structure. With numerical proverbs the emphasis falls on the last item, which is thus the point being made. In v. 19, that point is one of the most absorbing of human mysteries. The passage is often taken as a serious study of the natural world, but that is to labour the point somewhat. Quite simply, these two verses are marked by the very human emotion of *wonder:* the free-floating eagle, master of an element denied mankind; the grace and secrecy of the serpent's passage, silent and deadly; the trackless path of a ship in its progress. This is a device used in the "Theophany" of the Book of Job (38:1–42:6) with a theological purpose. Here the purpose is more human, as the author ponders the mystery of human sexuality, "The way of a man and a maiden". Clearly, the key to any valid understanding of these verses is the term "way", used four times as a unitive and comparative device. All these phenomena have a way proper to themselves, and the focal point is the "way" of sexual attraction.

This is a more open treatment of a theme popular with the authors of Proverbs—the incalculable. We have learned to live with many incomprehensibles, with many mysteries of the human world: what more mysterious than the magic that lies between the sexes? To Prov 30 it is clearly more than a biological trick—it is even an insight into the mystery of God. Having accepted many individual mysteries, cannot one accept the reality of mystery itself?

This idea of the "way" fascinated the authors of the book, as can be seen from the number of times it reoccurs: 14:12; 16:1–9, 25; 21:2. Normally it is presented as a direct statement, neither contested nor explained. Here it is more oblique, and far more open-ended for it leaves the initiative with the reader. As such it stands in contrast to the rest of this chapter, where a docile acceptance of the ineffability of God's "word" is prescribed: vv. 7–9 and 32–33.

As if in deliberate contrast—an artistic device, as it were—there follows in v. 20 an addition that misses the point. A sense of the banal follows on a sense of wonder, perhaps as an editorial emphasis? The woman depicted here, who approaches life as if it were a matter of "eating, and wiping one's mouth", demonstrates an indifference that is only semi-humourous. She has no moral religious conscience, and less moral perception. No mystery impinges upon *her* world. Life is a superficial occurrence, she sucks it dry and casts the rind away.

THE FOUR SMALL THINGS THAT ARE WISE. 30:24–28.

[24] Four things on earth are small,
but they are exceedingly wise:
[25] the ants are a people not strong,
yet they provide their food in the summer;
[26] the badgers are a people not mighty,
yet they make their homes in the rocks;
[27] the locusts have no king,
yet all of them march in rank;
[28] the lizard you can take in your hands,
yet it is in kings' palaces.

This, like the previous pericope, is a numerical proverb, and indeed a classic of the genre. It is quiet, restrained and yet reflective—typical of the best in Proverbs. The structure is doric, four parallel statements in sequence, based on the simple observation of natural phenomena, and no explicit moral or interpretation is drawn. It remains the task of the reader to apply each statement, and perhaps even the statement *as a whole,* to whatever personal situation may be involved. Unlike vv. 18–19, the formula has changed. It is no longer the suggestive "three things . . . and four . . ." but an unadorned statement that here we deal matter-of-factly with four phenomena that we must presume have something in common. This appears to be the antithesis of seeming inadequate size or power, and an achievement that is out of proportion. So having an initial advantage—or of course disadvantage—in life need not be all that decisive. Intelligence, work, courage, any combination of the qualities that go to make up "wisdom", can achieve a goal disproportionate to the beginnings. The human person, faced with the awesomeness of existence, may be weak, but can indeed change the environment.

This again may have had some tenuous connection with vv. 21–23, at least redactionally. With a negative assessment of great ends and small beginnings is contrasted the positive. There it was a case of "put a beggar on horseback"—a worldly-wise, humourous perception regarding inferiors who become superior. At first sight, a simple case of unjustified arrogance, and a realization that most people dislike someone who gets ahead without earning the promotion. Such people, having achieved an unearned authority, leave everyone else with the uneasy feeling that they are not prepared, by nature or training, to assume the role. Not so is the one who, from small beginnings, attains the purple by discipline.

What seems to be common to each example in vv. 24–28 is a certain quality, and this may well be the key to interpretation. The ant is industrious, the badger tenacious, the locust disciplined, the lizard adaptable. All of these qualities go to make up what is included in the term "wise". But it is by no means a closed classification—each verse is open to a different interpretation on the part of each reader, who may see *different* qualities in these creatures. There may also be the suggestion that one finds a mixture of qualities in every person, weak and strong, and one cannot validly judge a person's value, moral or physical, solely on the basis of appearance. Here also is mystery.

Appendix 3:
The Words of Lemuel. 31:1–9.

This, like most of the Book of Proverbs, is an instruction for life. Formally, it sets out to supply a manual for rulers, and it is concerned with inculcating *moral* virtues, and not administrative skills. The teaching is personalized, as so often in Proverbs, for effect and emphasis. The Aramaic influence evident in the text (for example, "son" in v. 2) suggests a late date.

A MANUAL FOR LEADERS. 31:1–9.

31 The words of Lemuel, king of
Massa, which his mother taught
him:
[2]What, my son? What, son of
my womb?
What, son of my vows?
[3]Give not your strength to women,
your ways to those who destroy
kings.
[4]It is not for kings,
O Lemuel,
it is not for kings to

drink wine,
or for rulers to desire
strong drink;
[5]lest they drink and forget what has
been decreed,
and pervert the rights of all the
afflicted.
[6]Give strong drink to him who is
perishing,
and wine to those in bitter distress;
[7]let them drink and forget their
poverty,
and remember their misery no
more.
[8]Open your mouth for the dumb,
for the rights of all who are left
desolate.
[9]Open your mouth, judge righteously,
maintain the rights of the poor and
needy.

The title to this short section is found in v. 1: "The words of Lemuel, king of Massa". The fact that there is no known king, of Massa or elsewhere, by the name of Lemuel adds to the probability that this text deals with a universalized instruction on dedication to one's duty in life. Also, none of the virtues inculcated are exclusive to rulers, they are valid for all, even if especially so for those in public service. As in the title of the first appendix (30:1) "massa" is best taken to mean an oracle or a solemn statement. The reference to his mother (1b) offers an interesting insight into the shared role of both parents in education, as in 10:1.

Technically, this is royal wisdom, instruction of an administrator or leader in the community. The threefold repetition of "what, my son?" in v. 2 serves as an emphatic opening to the exhortation. The unambiguous attribution of the teaching to the mother underlines the importance of the mother in education and formation. In Proverbs the "precepts of the father" seems to be a linguistic formula for "parental" instruction, as such; the mother plays an equal role: 1:8; 6:20; 10:1; 15:20; 29:15; 31:26. Normally, a scribe would not so address a ruler, he would not presume on such familiarity; so here the "maternal" form is a literary device. The rest of the chapter proceeds from negative to positive. In sequence is depicted the evil and folly of loose living for anyone who presumes to the role of leader in the community (vv. 3–7), and the value and wisdom of equitable and just administration, that is, doing one's job well. Verse 3 warns the reader against promiscuity. The image is that of a king who keeps a harem, and a recognition of the fact that this can be costly (the reference to "strength"), and can sap physical and moral resources. In this way a community leader can weaken his own authority, cause dissension (a warning against favouritism), and contribute to imbalance and disproportion in the community. This can gain nothing but the contempt of more reasonable people.

The second step in this exhortation is the presentation of drunkenness (vv. 4–7) in its effects. It distorts judgement, and that is the first vice, for once judgement is gone human competence is weakened. One becomes a servant of circumstances instead of a master. As the sage sees it, wine is a drug, therefore it behoves the sensible person to use it as such, with care. To someone who finds life really worthwhile and interesting it should not be necessary. Abused, it leads to a refusal, and an inability, to do one's job. There is no prohibitionism about this text—the idea would be alien to the society in which the sage lived—just a sensible awareness of the threshold where it ceases to be a good. Again, as in v. 3, it is less a *particular* vice than a general weakening of moral strength that is in question. Can one who is given to *any* debilitating habit stand for justice, or hold out against bribes, or be objective in judgements? This is the question, and not a particular weakness to which one may not be prone oneself.

But to be creative, a member of any community must represent more than an avoidance of vices; he must *assert* a special authority. In fact, this is brought out clearly by the opening formula in v. 8 and v. 9. This is necessary to bring about justice, to assert the right, to ensure equity especially for those who cannot pay for it and most need it—the natural victims of society. Here the actual legal system known to the author is in question (''judge'' in v. 9a), but the total perspective is, as is usual with a proverb, wider and more personalized.

Clearly, it is the sage's opinion that anything that obscures or fuddles one's judgement—sex or wine are given as examples—results in the loss of personality and the loss of human autonomy. This is especially to be deprecated in the case of those who have a social responsibility (note the reference to ''poor'', etc., in vv. 5–9).

Appendix 4:
The Ideal Woman. 31:10–31.

Like the previous section, and indeed like the editorial introduction of chapters 1—9, this last pericope is a late creation; certainly post-exilic, possibly second century B.C., as the Aramaic influence would suggest. The background is that of a middle-to-upper class family, typical of the genre, and it reflects the wisdom preoccupation with maturity, competence and success.

A WOMAN BEYOND PRICE. 31:10–31.

[10] A good wife who can find?
She is far more precious than jewels.
[11] The heart of her husband trusts in her,
and he will have no lack of gain.
[12] She does him good, and not harm,

all the days of her life.
[13] She seeks wool and flax,
and works with willing hands.
[14] She is like the ships of the merchant,
she brings her food from afar.
[15] She rises while it is yet night
and provides food for her
household
and tasks for her maidens.
[16] She considers a field and buys it;
with the fruit of her hands she
plants a vineyard.
[17] She girds her loins with strength
and makes her arms strong.
[18] She perceives that her merchandise
is profitable.
Her lamp does not go out at
night.
[19] She puts her hands to the distaff,
and her hands hold the spindle.
[20] She opens her hand to the poor,
and reaches out her hands to the
needy.
[21] She is not afraid of snow for her
household,
for all her household are clothed
in scarlet.
[22] She makes herself coverings;
her clothing is fine linen and purple.
[23] Her husband is known in the gates,
when he sits among the elders of
the land.
[24] She makes linen garments and sells
them;
she delivers girdles to the merchant.
[25] Strength and dignity are her clothing,
and she laughs at the time to
come.

[26] She opens her mouth with wisdom,
and the teaching of kindness is on
her tongue.
[27] She looks well to the ways of her
household,
and does not eat the bread of
idleness.
[28] Her children rise up and call her
blessed;
her husband also, and he praises
her:
[29] "Many women have done excellently,
but you surpass them all."
[30] Charm is deceitful, and beauty is
vain,
but a woman who fears the LORD
is to be praised.
[31] Give her of the fruit of her hands,
and let her works praise her in the
gates.

Stylistically, this is an acrostic poem, and it develops a theme that occurs frequently in the Book of Proverbs: 5:15; 12:4; 18:22—the "good wife", though in keeping with the style of these appendices the theme is generalized and transformed into a symbol. The structure is built up with great care: a personal appeal for attention (10–12) is followed by a portrait of one who is industrious, balanced and generous (13–20), possessed of a sense of duty (21–23) and more than usually competent (24–28). The whole is capped with an abstract poem of praise for such a paragon (30–31).

Taken in perspective, Proverbs is singularly even-handed in its descriptions of the sexes, and this is quite possibly due to the relative lateness of its composition. Fools, gossips and chatterers come from both sexes with neat impartiality, just as wise, provident and good men and women are well-balanced. Both have a constructive role to play in society. Sirach ends his book with the praise of "illustrious men"; true to its own overall structure, Proverbs ends with a praise of a wise woman. She has been the ideal all along—to some extent this has been the function of the personified Lady Wisdom. She stands, at the end of the quest, as an illustration of a fully integrated and human wisdom—and she has lost none of her allure. Thus the collection that is the Book of Proverbs ends with an engaging portrait. The careful construction is evidenced by the alphabetic sequence, a device frequently to be found in sapiential writings. To some extent this portrait is reminiscent of the introduction in the first nine chapters. In the Ideal Woman all wisdom comes together, secular and religious. In chapters 1—9 we were given an ideal of the search for wisdom; in these final verses we are given a prototype—the ideal fulfilled. The resourceful wife stands at the end as an image of all who have perfectly completed the wisdom adventure. Thus 31:10–31 is a "living" corollary to 1:1—9:18. There the ideal of a well-educated student, here a portrait of the person who is, next to God, most responsible for the formation of basic human values and is the source of the earliest influence for good.

This is not formally an inclusion, perhaps, but it does balance nicely, and this is precisely the sort of thing an Old Testament writer liked to resort to in giving unity to a collected work. It means that the portrait we find here is, of course, an ideal. Indeed, such qualities as are lavished on the figure in these verses are to be prized precisely because they are so hard to come by. And so is wisdom. The conclusion to the whole book is for the most part a long poem, international in tone, and it reflects the secular aspect of wisdom. However, in v. 30 the author has recourse to a traditional device, the "fear of Yahweh", to integrate this with yahwistic religion. It is the same device used in 1:7 to orientate the whole book.

The perfect woman of 31:10–31 is conceived of in terms of personified "Wisdom", as she was presented in the first nine chapters. Her distinguishing characteristic, there as here, is that she "fears the Lord". It is possible that with this key idea the Book of Proverbs has come full circle.

Bibliography

ON THE SAPIENTIAL LITERATURE.

R. E. Murphy. *Introduction to the Wisdom Literature of the Old Testament* (Old Testament Reading Guide 22). Liturgical Press, Collegeville, 1965.

General introduction to Hebrew poetry, and the sapiential literature of the Near East and of the Bible. It deals with the nature of wisdom and its general categories.

R. E. Murphy. *Seven Books of Wisdom.* Bruce Publishing Co., Milwaukee, 1960.

A more extended treatment of wisdom literature. It deals with each of the prominent sapiential books individually, giving a summary of the content of each, and of the theological preoccupation of each author.

R. B. Y. Scott. *The Way of Wisdom in the Old Testament.* Macmillan Co., New York, 1971.

A very full, detailed and well written introduction, dealing first with the nature, content and scope of the literature, in Israel and in the international context; and then with an analysis, mainly theological, of each of the more prominent books. He draws a clear distinction between conventional and intellectual traditions in wisdom.

R. B. Y. Scott. *Proverbs. Ecclesiastes* (Anchor Bible). Doubleday and Co., New York, 1965.

A shorter version of the preceding work can be found in the General Introduction (of 37 pages), giving an overall view in a short space. It also offers a short, useful bibliography.

O. S. Rankin. *Israel's Wisdom Literature. Its Bearing on Theology and the History of Religion.* Schoken Books, New York, 1969.

As the title suggests, this is a more specialized introduction, dealing particularly with the theological problems of theodicy, evil, and the individual, in the Old Testament and in Judaism.

Three other books of a general nature are

A.-M. Dubarle. *Les Sages d'Israel* (Lectio Divina 1). Editions du Cerf, Paris, 1946.

In spite of the date of publication, this is a remarkably fresh and imaginative interrogation of the wisdom books of the Old Testament. The author brings a poetic insight to what are essentially poetic books, and brings out the richness of the theological teaching of this particular biblical tradition. It includes a study of creation theology, and a concluding study of the wisdom influence on the New Testament writings.

E. Beaucamp. *Man's Destiny in the Books of Wisdom.* Alba House, New York, 1970.

A popular, readable analysis of the theological and spiritual content of the individual books of the wisdom literature, with an emphasis (as the title suggests) on the humanism and individual character and interest of the writings.

G. von Rad. *Wisdom in Israel.* S.C.M. Press, London, 1972.

A much more profound and intuitive treatment of wisdom itself, its nature and scope; its manner of functioning; and the theological polarities that dominate the literature and the tradition in Israel and in its universal application.

ON EXTRA-BIBLICAL LITERATURE.

James B. Pritchard. *Ancient Near Eastern Texts relating to the Old Testament.* Princeton, 3rd ed. with Supplement, 1969.

This is probably the classic source for English language scholarship of the texts from the ancient Near East that parallel or resemble the biblical texts. A scholarly translation from such varied literatures as Egyptian, Sumerian, Akkadian, Hittite, Babylonian and Assyrian, each document prefaced with a concise introduction.

Adolf Erman. *The Ancient Egyptians. A Sourcebook of their Writings.* (Harper Torchbooks), New York, 1966.

A translation of the important sources from Egypt. Within its limits (Egyptian literature only), it is possibly the best textbook available. It gives a very adequate outline of Egyptian history, and a useful introduction to the literature and life of early Egypt.

W. G. Lambert. *Babylonian Wisdom Literature.* Oxford, 1960.

The standard translation of the literature of ancient Mesopotamia. All the more important texts are translated, and commented on. There is a good introduction to the world of the sages who lived "between the two rivers".

Henri Frankfort & H. A. Frankfort. *Before Philosophy. The Intellectual Adventure of Ancient Man.* (Phoenix), Chicago, University Press, 1977.

This is a re-issue of a book first published in 1946, but it may well be the best general introduction to the thought and style of the extra-biblical literature. It deals with the major ideas and the development of thought of Egypt and Mesopotamia.

G. Pettinato. *The Archives of Ebla.* Doubleday, New York, 1981.

A new, and somewhat controversial, book on the "library" recently discovered at Ebla, in Syria. It illuminates a world that frequently seems to parallel that of the Biblical, and wisdom, texts.

ON THE SOCIAL DIMENSION OF WISDOM.

Walter Brueggemann, *In Man we Trust. The Neglected Side of Biblical Faith.* John Knox Press, Richmond, 1972.

A short, interesting treatment of the "secular" tradition of the Old Testament and its implications for contemporary theology.

Bernhard W. Anderson. *Creation versus Chaos. The Reinterpretation of Mythical Symbolism in the Bible.* Association Press, New York, 1967.

A fine treatment of the "creation theology" of the Old Testament, with an interesting section on the Priestly tradition and its influence on subsequent thought.

ON THE BOOK OF PROVERBS.

R. B. Y. Scott. *Proverbs. Ecclesiastes* (Anchor Bible). Doubleday, New York, 1965.

Provides an adequate, short introduction, and a very fine translation that makes the most use of linguistics and philology. The commentary itself is sparse.

D. Kidner. *The Proverbs. An Introduction and Commentary.* Tyndale Press, London, 1964.

A short introduction and commentary to the book. The introduction itself is very useful, the most valuable part of the book, and relatively extensive (56 pages). Particularly useful is the section that deals with "Subject Studies", which is a treatment of the most important themes dealt with in the Book of Proverbs.

A. Barucq. *Le Livre des Proverbes* (Sources Bibliques). Gabalda, Paris, 1964.
An excellent commentary, with an existential point of view that well suits the nature of wisdom literature. It is mostly interested in the theology and teaching of Proverbs. The first and last books are commented on directly, while the more amorphous central section is treated under the headings of the themes that dominate these collections.

W. McKane. *Proverbs. A New Approach.* S.C.M. Press, London, 1970.
As the title suggests, it is a new approach, dealing separately with the two dominant genres in the book, "instruction" and "sentence" literature. There is an excellent introduction to international wisdom, and a good translation. The commentary is a very full one.

L. Alonso Schökel. *Proverbios y Eclesiastico* (Los Libros Sagrados). Ediciones Cristiandad, Madrid, 1968.
A very good translation made by an author with a sense of poetry. The commentary as such is short, little more than notes on the text, but surprisingly rich in theological insights.

R. N. Whybray. *The Book of Proverbs* (Cambridge Bible Commentary). Cambridge University Press, 1972.
A short introduction and commentary. The introduction is well done, and useful for students. The translation is up to date, using the most recent discoveries in languages, and the commentary itself is concise.

STUDIES ON WISDOM AND PROVERBS.

There are a few adequate general studies on the structure and teaching of the Book of Proverbs.

R. N. Whybray. *Wisdom in Proverbs, the Concept of Wisdom in Proverbs 1—9* (Studies in Biblical Theology). S.C.M. Press, London, 1965.

This is a short and interesting study on the structure, origins and teaching of the first nine chapters of the book. It centres its analysis around the distinction of ten discourses, and the importance of the later redactional additions.

W. McKane. *Prophets and Wise Men* (Studies in Biblical Theology). S.C.M. Press, London, 1965.

An analysis of the particular character of wisdom, and a study of the confrontation between prophecy and wisdom. A very useful light on the theological position of the sapiential tradition in the Old Testament.